JEAN RAY LAURY

IMAGERY
ON FABRIC

a complete
SURFACE DESIGN **handbook**

updated and expanded - second edition

C&T PUBLISHING

Editor: Lee M. Jonsson
Assistant Editor: Annie Nelson
Technical Editor: Sally Lanzarotti
Copy Editor: Judith M. Moretz
Illustrator: John M. Cram
Book Design: John M. Cram
Cover Concept: Diane Pedersen
Cover Production: John M. Cram and Kathy Lee
All samples by Jean Ray Laury, unless otherwise noted.
Photographer: E. Z. Smith, unless otherwise noted.

The author and the publisher have made every effort to obtain permission to reproduce specific images for this book. Please contact the publisher for further information.

Library of Congress Cataloging-in-Publication Data

Laury, Jean Ray.
    Imagery on fabric : a complete surface design handbook / Jean Ray Laury. — Updated and expanded 2nd ed.
        p. cm.
    Includes bibliographical references and index.
    ISBN 1-57120-034-7
    1. Textile printing. 2. Transfer-printing. 3. Screen process printing. 4. Iron-on transfers.   I. Title.
    TT852.L38   1997
    746.6'2—DC21   97-23759
                                                        CIP

Published by C&T Publishing, Inc.
P.O. Box 1456
Lafayette, CA 94549

10   9   8   7   6   5   4   3   2   1

about copyright

While transfer methods make it simple and easy to copy almost anything, it is neither legal nor ethical to use copyrighted material without permission. To obtain permission, write to the publication or person, explain your intended use, and simply ask. Include a return card that requires only a signature; you will be more likely to get a response. I have never been refused permission to use copyrighted material. (But then, I've never asked Disney to let me print Mickey Mouse). It is unlikely that you would be given permission to use any commercially successful and familiar image. The purpose of the copyright is to protect the originator of the work, who should be the only one to have the right to use it or to profit by it. If copyrighted material is incorporated into any piece which will be exhibited or publicized, it will be important to have copyright permission.

Copyright-free publications let you select and use any image you like. And it is pretty simple to slip a roll of film into your camera and take your own pictures; then you are free to do whatever you like to them. To determine if a piece is copyrighted, first look for the © symbol. In publications, the entire book or magazine is covered by the copyright.

Copyrighting also helps you when you have a design which you would like to protect. Place the copyright symbol, plus your name and the year, on the work itself. Then, to register it, write for form VA at the Register of Copyrights, Library of Congress, Washington, DC 20559. There is a small registration fee and a relatively simple form to fill out.

caring for
YOURSELF AND THE
environment

Know the art materials you are working with, and read all information regarding their safe use and disposal. Non-toxic water-based paints and safe materials are recommended throughout this book, with just two exceptions. The light-sensitive methods (cyanotype, for example) have unique and special characteristics which can be achieved only with the use of some toxic chemicals. The second exception is the occasional use of solvents. Read all the information and consider the risks before determining which methods you will use.

Material Safety Data Sheets are available with any hazardous material you purchase. These identify for you exactly which elements are harmful, what precautions to follow, how to clean up and dispose of the materials, and how to respond to a mis-use of the product. Always request this sheet when you make a purchase so you have the information you need.

You can minimize disposal concerns by carefully estimating the amounts you will need. (Further information is given in the appropriate chapters.) When the data sheets talk about "shoveling up" spilled materials, we know they are talking about quantities vastly larger than what we use in home studios. The agencies I talked with all regarded home studio amounts as "minute" and "negligible." If you are making occasional, careful use of a product, it is unlikely you will encounter a problem. To work with it extensively or to teach the process, you must take greater precautions.

Never mix home and studio areas if you are working with any toxic materials. Allow no food, drink, or smoking in the work area. Keep measuring tools and mixing dishes for workroom use only and identify them so they will not find their way to the kitchen. Be particularly attentive to the use and storage of toxic materials, especially if you have small children around. Specific precautions are given in the chapter where there is a need for concern. See the Disposal of Hazardous Materials in Additional Help.

TABLE OF CONTENTS

acknowledgments

My warmest thanks to the artists who generously shared their information, knowledge, and finished pieces. They added both spirit and substance to this book. Susan Smeltzer and Lizabeth Laury were helpful and energetic when it mattered most. The editors at C&T were all enthusiastic and endlessly helpful. I thank especially Lee Jonsson, Annie Nelson, and Sally Lanzarotti for their remarkable attention to detail, and Diane Pederson and John Cram for their attentiveness to the lively and colorful design of this book.

To Carolyn Skei, Bobbie Smetherman, and Linda S. Miksch, my warmest thanks for the careful reading of parts of this manuscript.

And thanks to Frank for his culinary skills, without which I'd surely have perished.

introduction

In the magical world of image transfer, almost anything can be transferred or printed on cloth. Treasures from a family photo album, ferns, your child's drawing, your husband's parking ticket, a poem, or a snapshot of you at the Tower of London can all find their way onto fabric.

Astonishing new products and advances in transfer sheets allow inkjet prints to be made permanent on cloth and full-color copies to be transferred at home. The Polaroid® camera is also making a comeback with fiber artists. Along with technologically advanced methods, traditional ways of working are also included in this book—though designers have put them to new and innovative uses.

Safe, water-based, non-toxic paints and materials are used throughout this book. Gone are oil-based paints and thinners! When solvents or sensitizers are required (as in light-sensitive processes), they are clearly identified and procedures are carefully outlined. (A few processes offer no viable substitutes.)

My intent with *Imagery on Fabric* is to offer as comprehensive an array of processes as is feasible in one volume. That makes it possible for you to compare methods, and to find alternative ways of achieving a similar effect. There are constant crossovers (like screen printing with discharge). Options and possibilities pop up everywhere. I also wanted to share my experiences and experimentations, and to invite you to join the fun, work, and excitement. Included are clear outlines of what you need and step-by-step instructions.

Fiber artists and quilters from across the country generously and willingly added beauty, spirit, and clarity to this book. It is through their work that the processes come to life. You'll make your own changes, improvements, and variations as you work. But here, in one gigantic nutshell, is everything you need to know in order to begin.

Here is information on every technique I know for putting images onto cloth in a home studio. Step-by-step directions are given in every chapter, and each should be read from the beginning.

Reference Chart

You will find the chart on pages 6-7 remarkably helpful. It offers a quick summary of all the pertinent information regarding methods, which fabrics to use, permanence, suitability for children's use, safety, etc. Many craftswomen have posted this chart on the studio wall for easy referral.

Source List

Each process includes a source list of the specific products which may be used. Following each product is a number which refers you to an entry in the Resource Guide. The supplier may be a local store where you can find the product, or a mail-order source. Companies, addresses, and 1-800 numbers are included. A complete index speeds up the location of methods, artists, and products.

Additional Help

At the back of the book is a section called Additional Help. This includes descriptions or definitions, and information pertinent to the work. These references are indicated in <u>underlined</u> type.

Examples chosen for this book include simple initial projects, a few samples made by children, as well as some of the finest work being done by today's artists. You can plunge in at any level. I hope this book will guide you in a series of explorations and adventures.

USE THIS METHOD — IF YOU HAVE

USE THIS METHOD	Drawings (or copies of)	Childrens' art	Paper cut-outs, stencils	Natural forms: fish, leaves	Letters, words (or copies of)	A black and white copy of	A color copy of an original	A black and white copy of an original	A negative	A color slide or print	A black and white photo	Computer images	Polaroid film	Relief patterns: incised or carved	Graphic designs	Paintings	recommended fabrics	permanence on fabric
Fabric through black and white copy machine	*	*		*	*			*			*						cotton or silk, stabilized	hand washable; varies w/ copier
Transfer medium; bottled	*					*	*										cotton, silk	hand washable: do not dry clean or iron
Solvent transfer	*					*	*										natural fibers, test others	washable
Mending tape transfer	*					*	*										cotton, blends, silk	hand washable
Color laser copier heat transfer sheets		*		*	*			*		*	*					*	white or light cotton or blends	washable
Fabric through black and white laser printer				*								*					cotton, silk, blends; stabilized	hand washable; varies w/ printer
Dye transfer prints on black and white laser printer				*								*					65% or more synthetic	permanent when heat set
Canon Fabric Sheets: inkjet printer				*			*			*		*				*	provided	permanent, washable
Heat transfer sheets: inkjet printer		*		*		*	*			*		*					cotton, cotton-poly blend	washable, vinegar pre-wash
Dye transfer ribbon: dot matrix printer				*								*					65% or more synthetic	permanent when heat set
Fabric through a typewriter				*													any smooth fabric, stabilized	some are permanent, some wash out
Transfer crayon, rubbings or drawings	*	*											*				satin acetate, 65% or more synthetic	permanent on synthetic
Dye sticks			*	*									*				natural fibers, blends	permanent on natural fibers
Disperse dye on transfer paper			*	*	*												65% or more synthetic	washable
Disperse dye on copy	*			*	*	*											65% or more synthetic	hand washable
Quick screen: freezer paper or paper stencil			*		*										*		fabrics appropriate to paints or dyes	washable, follow paint directions
Photo silk-screen			*	*	*		*								*		fabrics appropriate to paints or dyes	washable, follow paint directions
Thermal imager	*	*			*	*									*		fabrics appropriate to paints or dyes	washable, follow paint directions
Cyanotype or Blueprint			*	*	*			*	*								cotton, silk, test others	washable, may fade, dry clean okay
Van Dyke or Brownprint			*	*	*			*	*								cotton, silk, test others	washable, may fade, dry clean okay
Kwik-Print			*	*	*			*	*								satin acetates and synthetics	wash or dry clean, cotton and silk retain some residue
Inko print			*	*	*			*	*								cotton, linen, natural fibers	permanent, cool wash, regular dry
Stamp print or block print			*	*										*	*		fabrics appropriate to paints or dyes	washable, follow paint directions
Monoprint																*	fabrics appropriate to paints or dyes	washable, follow paint directions
Leaf hammering				*													cotton, natural fibers	highly variable, test for permanence
Discharge liquid or powder	*		*	*													rayon, cotton, natural fibers	permanent
Polaroid transfer										*			*				cotton, silk, blends	hand washable, no abrasion

CHART

washing instructions	change in fabric	use with children	heat set	black and white or color	health hazards
hand wash, cool, air dry	no	w/ supervision	yes, after curing	black and white or color toner	
hand wash, cool, air dry	adds stiffness	no	varies	full color or black and white	
hand wash, cool, regular dry	no	no	yes	full color or black and white	solvents
hand wash, cool, line dry	slightly stiff	no	no	full color or black and white	
cool wash, max. 90°, no iron, air dry, no additives	adds stiffness	no	no	full color	
cool wash, air dry	no	w/ supervision	yes, after curing	black and white	
warm water, regular dry, iron okay	no	w/ supervision	yes	single colors	
cool wash, detergent w/color protection, normal dry	no	w/ supervision	no	full color	
cool wash, detergent w/color protection, normal dry	slightly stiff	w/ supervision	yes	full color	
warm water, iron okay	no	w/ supervision	yes	single colors	
cool wash, air dry	no	w/ supervision	advised	single colors	
warm wash, no bleach, line dry	no	w/ supervision	yes	limited range of color	
cool wash, air dry	no	w/ supervision	yes	limited range of color	
warm wash, regular dry	no	w/ supervision	yes	single colors (can be mixed)	if mixing powders
warm wash, regular dry	no	w/ supervision	yes	single colors (can be mixed)	
warm wash, regular dry	softens with washing	w/ supervision	yes	one color at a time	
warm wash, regular dry	softens with washing	no	yes	one color at a time	photo emulsion
warm wash, regular dry	softens with washing	w/ supervision	yes	one color at a time	
warm wash, no phosphates, no bleach	no	no	no	blue-green to indigo	light sensitive chemicals
warm wash, no phosphates, no bleach	no	no	no	brown	light sensitive chemicals
cool wash, cool dry	no	no	no	one color at a time	light sensitive chemicals
	no	no	no	one color at a time	light sensitive chemicals
warm wash, cool dry	not usually	yes	yes	any	
warm wash, cool dry	varies	w/ supervision	yes	any	
hand wash, cool, cool dry	no	w/ supervision	yes	varies	
warm wash, no bleach, regular dry	no	no	no	depends on fabric	bleach
cool water, air dry	slight stiffening	no	no	full color	photo chemicals

CHAPTER 1

copiers

Copiers, developed as office machines, have quickly been absorbed into artists' studios and rank high among their favorite appliances. Initially used to make multiples or to copy patterns, the copier was instantly applied to more versatile and exciting uses as artists cooked up ways to transfer designs directly to cloth. The arrival of color copiers revolutionized our way of working. Few advances have influenced and transformed surface design more than copiers. This chapter covers a variety of methods for transferring images onto fabric using copiers.

general information for using copiers
black and white copiers
color laser copiers

GENERAL INFORMATION FOR USING COPIERS

All copy machines deposit toner (dry ink) onto a sheet of paper and "set" it with heat. When freshly printed copies are stacked, ink may lift off, or transfer, from one sheet to another. For the artist who wants to transfer images, this tendency to lift off can be enhanced in various ways.

Transferring images is a simple, direct, and inexpensive way to work, allowing photographic results without a <u>darkroom</u>. It is easy to adjust, retouch, or trim a copy to eliminate the background. Or select one face or person out of a group picture, eliminating all the rest. With this method an archenemy can be annihilated with a clip of your scissors, or a spouse's "ex" can be removed from the scene! Snip out your own portrait (paper-doll fashion), and place yourself on a tropical beach or at the North Pole. Plant yourself on a surfboard, join the Bloomsbury group, or seat yourself in George Washington's boat as he crosses the Delaware. This cut-and-paste is the adventurous and exciting part of copy transfer.

image reversal

All one-step transfer processes result in images that are <u>reversals</u>. A copy, placed face down on fabric for transfer, will produce a reverse or "mirror" image of the original. The Tower of Pisa, leaning to the left in your original, will simply lean to the right when transferred. A photo of your right-handed daughter playing her guitar will be noticeably affected, as she now strums with her left hand.

You can work with an image where reversal doesn't matter (as in some photographs, but not lettering), or copy the original in mirror-image. To do this, copy your image onto a <u>transparency</u>, then flip the transparency in the copy machine to produce a reverse copy. The Tower of Pisa in the final transferred image will once again lean to the left and the guitarist will be right handed. Use a computer or copier which has a mirror-image option, or use a slide or color transparency and project it backwards when you make a copy.

running fabric
THROUGH THE copier

Many fiber artists feel compelled to run fabric through their copiers. The directness is exciting, but the machines may reveal their prima donna hearts and get petulant. It helps to have access to your own copy machine. I've copied on cloth extensively, and initially I kept my left hand at the electric outlet ready to unplug instantly if a problem surfaced. Now I no longer feel any concern.

You should know how to remove a paper from your copier and understand its basic functions (or have someone at hand who does) before feeding it this unusual, high-fiber diet. Some machines are sensitive to changes in page thickness, and may reject your first efforts.

Machines range in temperament from tolerant to persnickety. None of them like printing on fabric, and may balk or jam the laminated sheet. This is not disastrous. Jams most often occur after a sheet is printed but before it moves through the heat set and expulsion steps.

Open the machine, reach in, pull out the offending sheet, and discard it. Take care not to tear a sheet, leaving threads behind. A machine may accept one sheet and reject the next, or it may reject a stabilized sheet at the feeding mechanism. If this happens, turn the sheet and try the other edge first, or press it again to make sure it is flat. If the copier still rejects it, try a lighter-weight fabric.

Fabric choice affects the ease and success of transfer. Satin, chintz, glazed cotton, and similarly smooth woven fabrics give clearer, more detailed results than nubby or rough fabrics. The filler or sizing in some glaze <u>fabric finishes</u> will wash out, removing ink as it goes. All-cotton or silk fabrics work for most transfers, but test fabrics for permanence and washability. Select fabrics without surface treatments.

Both permanence and washability of copies on cloth vary. I've copied onto fabric using my Canon 2700® copier and, later, a Mita CS-1475®; the copies were permanent, even when I ran them through the washing machine with detergent (worst scenario treatment). Some designers report that their prints washed out entirely. Variables affecting colorfastness include curing time, fabric and finishes, heat setting, and the temperature at which the machine sets the toner (which differs among machines, and even models). To improve color permanence, dry the prints for a day, cover with paper before <u>heat setting</u> (or the iron may pick up the toner), then test wash.

Since fabric finishes affect printing and permanence, use <u>untreated fabric</u> or <u>PFP fabric</u> which has been "prepared for print." To run it directly through a machine, the fabric must have some body. Stabilize or laminate it by using any of these materials: iron-on <u>freezer paper</u>, glue sticks, <u>spray adhesive</u>, or spray starch.

Using Freezer Paper to Stabilize Fabric

Heat set to fabric, iron-on freezer paper adds enough body to make the fabric paper-like. It is easily applied or removed, and leaves little or no residue.

Cut the freezer paper and fabric (muslin, silk, or a similar-weight, light-colored fabric) about an inch larger than paper size, aligning paper to the fabric grain. Place fabric on ironing board, position freezer paper (plastic-side down), and heat set with a medium hot iron, securing the edges carefully. Trim to exact size of paper (8$\frac{1}{2}$" x 11") using a paper cutter or rotary cutter. Leave no loose threads. Laminated sheets will sometimes curl toward the fabric side. Flatten them by running the iron over the paper side just before inserting a sheet into the machine. Freezer paper is re-usable.

Using Glue Stick to Stabilize Fabric

Five or six glue-stick lines across the copy paper will also hold the fabric adequately. When printing, observe where the grabbers make contact with the paper to pull it through; it is essential that the paper-fabric bond be firm in that area. The leading edge and the end must both be well-adhered. A few additional lines of glue across the central part of the sheet should be enough.

Using Spray Adhesives to Stabilize Fabric

Spray adhesives, used to join paper to fabric, are more difficult to handle. Avoid breathing the spray; work outdoors. Spray provides a good, smooth contact but affects the hand of the fabric. Spray onto the copy paper, not the fabric.

Using Spray Starch to Stabilize Fabric

Spray starch adds enough body and stiffness to a fabric to make it printable, especially for a typewriter or copier. It is relatively easy to use, and you can stiffen the leading edge more heavily than the rest. Remember, however, that when you rinse the fabric, some of the toner will wash away with the dissolved starch. A copy machine which rejects laminated fabric may accept this thin, starched sheet, but it must be rigid enough not to crumple as it is pulled through.

WHAT YOU NEED

Original artwork or a good copy
Copier
PFP fabric (laminated with freezer paper or stiffened)
Iron and board
Optional:
Paint, dye sticks, or marking pens

THE PROCESS

1. Stabilize the PFP fabric. Leave no loose threads.
2. Run a test copy of your art through the copier to be sure it is clear. Adjust the size and darkness as desired.
3. Feed the prepared fabric into the machine through the tray or manual feed slot. Keep a finger on the Print button; copiers seem more eager to expel the fabric sheet when another print is coming right behind it. (It is like being pushed in line; it does keep you moving!)
4. When the print emerges, dry it for several hours to one day, longer in damp weather. Remove stabilizer backing, if used.
5. When dry, cover with paper and heat set. Then test for washability.
6. Add color with direct painting, dye sticks, or marking pens. See pages 55-56 and 58-59.

SOURCE LIST

Freezer paper, 5

PFP fabric, 38

Using Collages in the Copier

When copying a collage, lines will sometimes appear where the cut edge of one paper overlaps another. To avoid this, glue any cut edges for better contact, or weight the collage after it is placed face-down on the copy machine to flatten it and eliminate lines. If lines persist, you may need to cover them with a correction fluid made especially for copiers.

TROUBLESHOOTING FOR RUNNING FABRIC THROUGH COPIERS

Problem: Laminated fabric jams or stalls in the copier.
Solution: Open the machine and carefully pull the sheet out as you would for any paper jam. Use lighter-weight fabric or a different method.
Problem: Prints wash out.
Solution: Dry for a longer period. Heat set at a higher temperature. Try another copier (an older one). Use fabric with no surface finish.

Ritva

Ritva was printed by running silk (backed with freezer paper) through the black and white copier. Before the freezer paper was removed, color was touched-in with Caran d'Ache® watercolors.

It requires time and effort to develop skill in copy transfer. Don't expect immediate success. You'll develop a feel for the method, as have the many designers who work with it extensively and successfully. Remember that copiers and the temperatures at which toners are set affect ease of transfer. Allow a full day before laundering.

BLACK AND WHITE COPIERS

Fabric copies are rarely as black as paper copies, so be sure to work from art that has as much contrast as possible. Make several progressively darker copies until you achieve the strongest possible black-on-white copy from which to print your fabric. If lines are not dark and clear, try another copier. Always use a full-size piece of <u>stabilized fabric</u>. If you can't bear to waste the fabric, print two small images at one time.

Only opaque lines copy clearly. Lead pencil or blue pencil work poorly, so if you wish to use either, darken the copy or trace over it with a marker. Adjusting the copy machine to a darker setting gives a blacker line, but eventually the background begins to pick up toner. The density of the black may be affected by the age and condition of the machine, how it is set, or the toner itself. Some brands of copiers deposit more toner than others, so find the one which works best for you.

A first photographic enlargement on a copier is made directly from an original. As the images expand, the clarity of the print diminishes further. In second <u>generation copies</u>, solid areas break down into patterns. To retain the clarity of the original photo, have an enlargement made from the <u>negative</u>. Using the "photo" option available on some copiers will also help to some extent.

Add color to black and white prints by using permanent markers, dye transfer, transfer <u>crayons</u>, or <u>dye sticks</u>. <u>Textile paints</u> or <u>airbrush inks</u> can be used to create soft watercolor effects or a bright graphic look.

Printing Single Colors on the Black and White Copier

Colored toners, available to replace black toner in copy machines, can be transferred to fabric using the same methods as those for black toner. Many copy shops will change the cartridge color at your request. Brown toner gives a sepia effect to a photograph. Blue, red, and green toner can be used to create their own unique effects.

Patricia Kennedy-Zafred
Eloquence, 22" x 16½"
photo: Tom Little

Using multiple images of one of her photographs, the artist ran the picture through a black and white copier to make duplicates on acetate. By cutting, and sometimes layering colored fabrics between the white ground and the acetate, she varied the images and added visual accents. Machine stitching and threads enrich the surface.

Lura Schwarz Smith
Seams a Lot Like Degas, 48" x 52"
photo: Mellisa Karlin Mahoney

Lura paged through a book of Degas' pastel drawings to do her sketches. Once her full-size pencil sketches were completed (using a purple Prismacolor Pencil®), she ran them through a black and white copier, fitting the drawings onto 11" x 17" sheets. The result was a gray print, resembling a charcoal sketch. She then hand colored the faces, arms, and backs using thinned Versatex for a watercolor effect. Finished parts were hand appliquéd to the pieced panel. The transition from hand-painted areas to pieced patterns was reinforced with geometric shapes that spilled from background to foreground to create an overall design.

Arturo Alonzo Sandoval
To Honor Those Who Came Before
28" x 36" x 5"
photo: M.S. Rezny Photography

This quilt is Arturo's comment on the arrival of the Portuguese and Spanish in America. To a Styrofoam® base covered with reflective Mylar® he added sheets of acetate which had been imaged in a copier. Steps at the left, in this birds-eye view of a Mayan temple, descend the 5" depth of the piece. Black AstroTurf®, reminiscent of lava, edges the piece, and hundreds of plastic skeletons represent the loss of life. The acetate, perforated with the machine stitching and monofilament thread, is held in place with a layer of tulle.

Melissa Holzinger and
Wendy Huhn
Still Life Balancing Act, 60" x 47"
photo: David Loveall
Photography, Inc.

Collaborators Melissa and Wendy created the complex patterns in their quilt using an entire array of methods. They ran some of their figures and cut-outs through a black and white copier and hand-painted them with watercolors, acrylic paints, and markers. For heat setting the artists used an Elna Press® for twenty seconds. Color copies of the legs and heads, which make up the pedestal, as well as the remarkable collection of vegetables, screws, bags, coffins, saints, and chilies, which overflow it, are adhered to Wonder-Under® and then adhered to a second piece of fabric. The shapes were cut out and applied to the backing with Weld-Bond®, which adheres well to sprayed or "fixed" fabrics. The fish at the bottom are edged in the black felt, which was used as a foundation fabric. Airbrushing, hand stitching, computer printing, beading, and industrial quilting completed the panel.

Wendy Huhn
Detail of *Wife Wanted*
photo: David Loveall
Photography, Inc.

Wendy uses almost every technique at hand to produce her wonderfully funny wall pieces. In *Wife Wanted*, she first ran 9" x 12" pieces of fabric through her black and white copier to print the many dolls and figures. The central figure of a man was photocopied (in black toner), applied to Wonder-Under, and adhered to the collage. Because of a tendency for toners to migrate with fixative sprays, she prefers to heat set only using an Elna Press. The womens' figures were copied, applied to

Wonder-Under, adhered to another cloth, and attached to the background with Weld-Bond. The figures were hand-painted with acrylic paint (permanent) or Caran d'Ache watercolors which required "setting" with Krylon®. Once the panel was assembled, the artist decided that the central cloud pattern, printed with blue toner on a black and white copier, needed to be strengthened. Using a scalpel she cut freezer-paper stencils to protect the painted areas while adding a checkerboard pattern to the clouds. The black lines, which add depth to the layered images, were hand-painted.

transfer medium

Transfer medium is a thick, non-toxic liquid which can be painted onto black and white or color copies to facilitate their transfer to fabric. Transfer mediums are made specially for this purpose though the thicker transparent extender base used in screen printing will also work. Clay-coated pages from magazines or flyers can be transferred, since the ink can be lifted off the paper. Glossy or shiny pages work less well than matte or flat prints. So many different kinds of inks, coatings, varnishes, and finishes are now used on paper that it is difficult to predict which can be transferred. Do not apply the medium directly to original photographs—only to copies or prints. All transfer mediums change the hand of the fabric, adding slight stiffness.

Because photo images have clear areas where background (white) shows through, a transfer to dark fabric is not satisfactory. To retain clarity and have a dark background, transfer the image to a white fabric first. Cut this image out and stitch or adhere it to the dark fabric.

Bottled Transfer for Color or Black and White Copies

Directions come with each medium and, while all are similar, there are variations of which you must be aware.

Read all precautions for each product.

WHAT YOU NEED

A clear copy of original
Transfer medium
Wax paper (or clear wrap)
Brayer or rolling pin
Foam applicator or brush
PFP fabric on which to print
Paper towel
Iron and board
Press cloth
Sponge

THE PROCESS

1. Make a copy of your artwork or photograph (color or black and white).
2. Place any smooth PFP fabric over wax paper or clear wrap on a flat surface. It may be helpful to pin the fabric (for example, on an ironing board) to hold it smooth and taut.
3. Cut out the portion of the copy you wish to transfer, trimming to the edge and leaving a tab for handling. Place it face up on a second piece of wax paper.
4. Coat the copy with an even layer of transfer medium, 1/16" to 1/8" thick, which almost hides the image. Apply with a 1" brush or foam applicator, or a credit card.
5. Carefully lift the wet print by the tab and place the coated side down on the fabric.
6. Cover with wax paper or paper towel. To remove any air bubbles press with a brayer or rolling pin (very lightly) or by hand (very firmly) from the center out to the edges. When the paper backing of the print begins to wet through, run the brayer over all layers again.
7. Let dry 24 hours. Curing time is critical, and may take longer in high humidity.
8. Cover with a press cloth and heat set using a dry iron at medium setting. Heat setting depends upon the specific transfer medium. Some products, such as Picture This, do not require this step.
9. Remove the backing paper by gently sponging with water and rubbing to reveal a mirror image of the original. Or, place a damp sponge on the paper for several minutes to loosen it. If it is stubborn, let it dry, re-wet, and repeat.
10. When print is clean—when all backing paper has been rubbed off and the image is visible and clear—rub a few drops of the transfer medium into the image with your finger to seal it.

SOURCE LIST

Aleene's®, 3, 4, 16, 34

Picture This™, 3

PVC glue, 5

Stitchless Fabric Glue, 3, 34

Transfer-It, 3

Transfer Medium Decal

In addition to the process to reverse the image mentioned in the beginning of this chapter, it is also possible to make a decal of a copied image using any of the bottled transfers. The decal will be reverse-transferred, so it will read "right." This method is useful for transferring lettering or maps, but requires two layers of medium, so the finished piece will be thicker and glossier. It is easier to remove the backing paper, and no heat is required for the transfer. The finished piece should not be put in a dryer.

WHAT YOU NEED

A clear copy of original
Transfer medium
Wax paper (or clear wrap)
Brayer or rolling pin
Foam applicator or brush
PFP fabric on which to print
Paper towel

THE PROCESS

1. Brush a light coat of the transfer medium onto the printed side of your untrimmed copy and let it dry for two hours.
2. Add a second coat and dry for 24 hours.
3. Soak the coated paper in water for several minutes, then place it face down on wax paper over a hard surface.
4. Separate the paper copy from the transfer medium film by moistening and rubbing it gently, leaving a thin flexible film of "set" medium with ink on it.
5. Blot, dry, and trim edges of film.
6. Place face down on wax paper. Coat the back with more medium and, while wet, place it painted side down on the fabric for transfer.
7. Press with brayer or rolling pin.
8. If transfer medium oozes out the edges, remove it with a damp cloth. The transferred image will be oriented the same as the original.

Joan Schulze
Water Music, 49¹/₂" x 59¹/₂"
photo: Sharon Risedorph

Joan's panel includes many photocopied images which were transferred. She prefers PVC glue (which is archival) to the lighter-weight Picture This and the heavier Stitchless. The consistency of PVC allows for the use of different spreaders, foam brushes, bristle brushes, or wood strips, to create varying surfaces. The red area in her panel was transferred from a copied collage. The artist also presents color images in an unusual way. She color-prints both sides of a sheet of paper and then places one image face down on the fabric with PVC transfer. The second image is partially scraped away to create a layered effect, with one image emerging from beneath another.

solvent transfer

This transfer method uses solvents to dissolve black and white or color toner off a copy, along with pressure to adhere it to fabric. All solvent transfers produce reverse prints of the copy used. Fresh copies tend to release their inks more readily than older ones. It is easier to handle small prints than full pages, so if several images are grouped on one page, cut them apart and transfer them individually. As both solvents and inks vary, only experimentation and a process of elimination will determine the most satisfactory combination. Copies from older machines tend to transfer more readily.

WARNING: All solvents are potentially hazardous. Protect yourself: read all labels on the products you buy and observe all precautions. If ingested, solvents are highly toxic. Avoid breathing the fumes by working outdoors or in a hood-ventilated area, and wash hands after contact. Protective neoprene gloves, goggles, and masks are recommended. Keep away from children. Do not allow smoking, open flames, or food anywhere near open containers or the work area. Purchase solvents in small amounts and use directly from the can to avoid leftover disposal.

Observing all precautions for solvents, you can work comfortably. It is not necessary to become overly anxious about it, but you must protect yourself. Occasional use is unlikely to cause any problems, but for extensive use, extra care must be taken.

WHAT YOU NEED

A clear copy of original

Solvent
(descriptions to follow, page 18)

Clean, smooth cardboard
(about 10" x 12", not corrugated)

Masking tape

Cotton or flannel
(about 6" square)

Burnisher
(or an old spoon or iron)

Fabric on which to print
(anything not melted by solvent)

Iron and board

Optional:
Permanent markers, crayons,
or textile paints

THE PROCESS

1. Select your solvent.
2. Select a linear design or pattern of alternating dark and light. Large areas of black or gray do not transfer clearly.
3. Cut a piece of fabric larger than your design, iron it smooth, and place it right side up on the cardboard. Tape all edges so the fabric is perfectly smooth.
4. Place your copy face down on the fabric and tape it at the top only, to form a hinge.
5. Take copy, fabric-covered cardboard, solvent, cloth, and burnisher to an outdoor work table, or work with good ventilation, e.g., a hooded fan.
6. Wearing rubber or neoprene gloves, saturate a small soft cloth with solvent by holding the folded cloth over the opened container spout and tipping the can to moisten the cloth. Immediately replace the cap.
7. Wipe the cloth over a small section of your copy. (You will be moistening the back side.) The paper will soak up the solvent and appear to be wet or translucent. Immediately burnish that area, using the bowl of an old spoon or any similar hard, smooth object. This helps press the ink from copy to fabric.
8. Peek under a corner to see how the copy is transferring, but do not lift the entire sheet.
9. When the transfer is complete, remove the paper from the fabric. Air dry and heat set.
10. Add colors, using permanent markers, fabric crayons, or any water-based textile paints.

SOURCE LIST

Acetone, 1, 5

Citra-Solve®, 9

Goo Gone™, 3, 5

Mineral Spirits, 1, 5

Strip-Eze® Varnish Remover, 5

Turpenoid®, 1, 5, 22, 34

Heat Setting

Solvent transfers should be heat set to help assure permanence. Let the fabric dry thoroughly, then press the reverse side with a medium hot iron. Actually, I press directly on the print, but it must be completely dry (allow a full day). If the ink is even slightly damp, it may smear or stick to the iron. Solvent transfers are permanent. If parts of a design are transferred separately, earlier transfers should be heat set or protected so they are not dissolved by later ones which may overlap.

Following are some of the most common of the many solvents available:

Turpenoid (Odorless Paint Thinner)

This synthetic turpentine substitute can be used in the transfer process. It is less hazardous than gum turpentine. Use with good ventilation and wash your hands thoroughly when finished.

Mineral Spirits

Mineral spirits work well for copy transfer but should be used outdoors because of the fumes. Observe all precautions. In the book *OvereXposure* by Susan D. Shaw and Monona Rossol, mineral spirits are described as a moderately toxic solvent when inhaled or put in contact with the skin, but highly toxic if ingested.

Linda Pool
Details of *Chris's College Quilt*
photo: Linda Pool

Acetone

Acetone is only slightly toxic with any normal exposure, but special care must be taken to prevent any possibility of eye contact. Safety goggles are recommended even if you wear prescription glasses. Work outdoors to avoid fumes and because acetone is extremely flammable. Most households have other liquids around which contain acetone (some nail polish removers, lighter fluids, cleaners, etc.), and all offer some degree of success for transfer.

Citra-Solve

Citra-Solve is a citrus-based solvent which has an orange-oil odor and somewhat less toxicity than many other solvents. It transfers most readily with a hot iron. It is available in some hardware, health food, and alternative supply stores.

Strip-Eze Varnish Remover

Strip-Eze Varnish Remover is a powerful, thick solvent which works well, though precautions must be observed. With Strip-Eze you have more time to work.

Colorless Blenders

Xylene®-based markers are colorless blenders which work well for solvent transfer, though good ventilation is a must. They are very convenient and there is no danger of spills.

solvent transfer
WITH ironing

Solvent transfer can sometimes be accomplished using an iron to replace burnishing. Some designers prefer it, as heat facilitates the transfer, and even pressure can be applied to a large area. Take the iron outside and follow instructions given in The Process on page 17.

TROUBLESHOOTING FOR SOLVENT TRANSFER

Problem: No transfer occurs.

Solution: Try another copy or another copier.

Use fresh solvent. Use more heat.

Problem: Runny-looking prints on fabric.

Solution: Use less solvent.

Work faster. Paper should be moistened, not soaked.

Problem: Pale prints or loss of detail.

Solution: Use a darker or fresher copy.

Use an original with greater contrast, and try again.

Use more solvent.

Burnish with more elbow grease.

Details may be too fine to transfer to fabric.

Problem: Your print is spotty (some dark areas, some light).

Solution: Apply solvent evenly and burnish smoothly.

Make sure your work surface is smooth and fabric is free of any finish.

Problem: The image is misaligned or double.

Solution: Tape the copy and the fabric to keep them from moving.

Problem: Your transfer has a pattern of lines over the surface.

Solution: Use a smoother burnishing tool—the bowl of a spoon, not the edge.

Betsy Nimock
The Immigrant, 42" x 43"
Detail of *The Immigrant*
photo: Betsy Nimock

Betsy combines the remnants of a bold and graphic old quilt with flags and a portrait that symbolizes the immigrant women in the United States. The quilt block behind the portrait suggests a halo of woman's work. The portrait is charcoal enhanced, a photographic treatment common from Civil War times to the early twentieth century. Betsy applied the photo to the panel using a fabric glue. The thirty-five star flag is solvent transferred to cloth and burnished with Hunt's Speedball® Baren #4139. This small tool, made for hand printing, has a non-stick base and is helpful in applying steady pressure.

Johnnene Themean Maddison
Turn Around and You're Four, 34" x 59"
Detail of *Turn Around and You're Four*
photo: John Tamblyn

Johnnene used a single ink
drawing from her sketch book as the
basis for this panel. After making a
number of photocopies, some of
them reversals, she transferred them
to cloth with Citra-Solve, adding
the chair sketch to complete her
composition. Some transfers
overlapped, creating a transparent
effect. Color was added with colored
pencils and the panel was heat set.
The trees were thermal image prints.

Elia Woods,
Crystal's Quilt, 60" x 44"
photo: Jenny Woodruff

Elia, who works with an Indian
Youth Empowerment Project
through a non-profit group,
photographed the children as they
spelled 'I love you' with their
bodies. She then transferred copies
of the photos to silk using Citra-
Solve. The transfer areas were
painted over with Deka® silk resist,
as were designs on other blocks,
and all were then silk painted.

Betsy Nimock
Blood Sacrifice, 30" x 40"
photo: Betsy Nimock

In one of her forays through an antique shop, Betsy found a wonderful old photo of these sisters. In photocopying, the girls' heads were inadvertently cut off. That evoked images of the Mayan sacrifices of maidens, since Betsy saw the sisters as also having been sacrificed—"packaged" for consumption. The artist copied the black and white photo on a color copier, exaggerating the amount of yellow in the top panel, red in the center, and green at the bottom. These prints were then solvent transferred to China silk using mineral spirits. The image on the right is a painting by the artist, photocopied and transferred.

B.J. Adams
Outline on Asphalt, 26" x 32"
photo: Breger and Associates

Small guns were photocopied on paper, then before the toner set, they were transferred to poly-satin using heat and pressure only (no solvent). Letters were stamped onto paper and manipulated on a copier to achieve the desired size. From the paper they were heat set onto the fabric and then embroidered. A soldering iron was used to burn the holes in the panel and oil pastel was used to outline the form of a body.

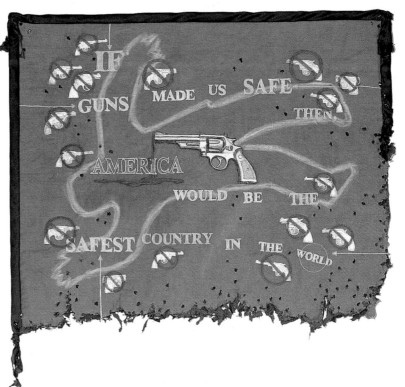

transfer BY ironing (NO SOLVENT)

Occasionally copies can be transferred to fabric simply by ironing. It is worth a try. Place a fresh copy face down on the fabric and press with a hot iron for about 30 seconds. Lift a corner to check, and continue ironing if the image has not transferred. This method is unpredictable. If it does not work, try another copier or use a heat press. Transferability is dependent upon variables (unknown to me), and even two copiers of identical model may perform differently.

improvised transfer methods

Improvised transfer methods are those which are adapted to transfer but were not designed for this purpose, such as iron-on mending tape and contact paper.

Mending Tape Transfer (for Black and White Copies)

Polyester-cotton mending tape has a heat-transferable adhesive coating which can pick up toner (or ink) from a copy and transfer it to fabric. It is available in notions departments, fabric shops, or dime stores as Bondex by Wrights or Mending Patches by Coats and Clark (both available in strips or patches). IronOn Patches from Penn are low-heat transfers. This method is subject to the variations in toners and copiers and will require experimentation. The process is described in Marjorie Croner's excellent book *Fabric Photos*.

SOURCE LIST

Coats and Clark® Mending Patches, 3, 4

Penn IronOn Patches, 3, 4

Wrights Bondex®, 3, 4

WHAT YOU NEED

A black and white copy

Iron-on mending tape

PFP fabric on which to print

Iron and board

THE PROCESS

1. Place iron-on mending tape over a copy of your image.
2. Transfer image to mending tape by using an iron at wool setting for about 30 seconds. Do not use added pressure. Peel.
3. Place fabric on which you are going to print on a flat, smooth ironing surface.
4. Place the mending tape (with the copy transferred to it) face down on the fabric.
5. Transfer image to fabric with an iron, at a higher temperature. Iron one minute, at cotton setting, with pressure.

The method requires practice, but many designers work with it successfully. Copiers vary and affect the amount of heat and pressure needed to transfer an image. Newer copy machines work less well for this purpose; trying several different copiers may be helpful. The final transfer on fabric is permanent and washable. Any textile paint or permanent fabric marker can be used to add color.

Ritva

Solvent transfer painted with thinned Versatex.

TROUBLESHOOTING FOR MENDING TAPE TRANSFER

Problem: There is a poor transfer from copy to mending tape.

Solution: Use more heat (try the cotton setting).
Remove the paper before it cools.
Try another copier.

Problem: You can't separate the mending tape from the paper.

Solution: Insert a tab between tape and copy when you stack them.

Problem: There is poor transfer from mending tape to fabric.

Solution: Use more pressure to aid in the transfer.
Use higher heat, increasing the ironing time.

Problem: The mending tape sticks to the fabric.

Solution: Reheat, then pull the mending tape off before it cools.

Problem: Lines or streaks appear in the transferred image.

Solution: Pull the mending tape in one long pull, not in steps.

Contact Paper Transfer

As an alternative, <u>contact paper</u> can also be used to pick up the toner from a black and white copy. It is burnished over the print, then peeled off, lifting the toner. The contact paper is placed sticky side up on a firm smooth work surface and fabric is placed on top. Both are taped in place. Working outside or with good ventilation, wipe a small cloth moistened with solvent over a portion of the fabric. <u>Burnish</u>. Dampen an adjacent area and continue until the entire print has been transferred.

Jackie Vermeer
Flower, 7" x 7"

The flower shown here was transferred using contact paper and solvent. What appears to be pencil strokes are the lines created from the burnishing tool.

Joan Tobin
Cat Pillow, 7" x 7" x 24"

Mending tape transfer was used to transfer an image of Joan's cat to a pillow. She made a transparency (on the copier) of her photo so she could flip it to produce a mirror-image copy. The two mirror-imaged cats form a symmetrical design, interrupted with patterned strips and another image in the center, all machine sewn in place.

Jackie Vermeer
Happy Birthday, Mom, 45" x 45"

Transfers with contact paper as well as heat transfers for inkjet and color laser copiers combined in this photo-filled traditional block pattern.

COLOR LASER COPIERS

Many fabric and fiber artists began by using the color laser copier as a means of recording, cataloging, or collecting the visual reminders of special events. This new focus for photography is seductive—often the mere mechanical reproduction of a color picture offers a satisfying result. As the process becomes more familiar, altered images become one more element to be manipulated in the composition.

Color prints dazzle us with vivid realism. When printed on heat transfer sheets, they offer us a full-color photographic process which can be used directly on cloth. The prints can be transferred with a heat press or with an iron. Unimaged transfer sheets can be used to seal inkjet prints. Some fiber artists incorporate the paper copies into their work, while others prefer solvent and medium transfers. A new spray transfer bypasses the use of papers and solvents.

I know a fiber artist who runs a print shop (a rare combination), and after ironing her fabric onto freezer paper, she ran it through the automatic bypass of her color laser copier. The first experiment came out too pale, so it was necessary to darken the image. Perhaps eventually this will become an option—at present, it is not.

Ritva

A color laser copier transfer sheet applied with an iron to cotton fabric. These transfers require white or light fabric for background.

heat transfer sheets
FOR color copy transfer

Transfer sheets are polymer-coated papers which can be fed into a color laser copier, and then permanently heat set to cloth. The transfer colors are vivid and the process is not difficult.

SOURCE LIST

WHAT YOU NEED

Transfer paper
<u>Original</u> image
(photo, drawing, map,
document, slide)
Access to color laser copier
<u>PFP fabric</u> to receive transfer
Heat press or <u>iron and board</u>

THE PROCESS

1. Copy your original onto the special transfer paper through a color laser copier.
2. Cut away excess transfer material surrounding the image.
3. Preheat fabric by pressing with a dry iron to facilitate transfer and remove excess moisture.
4. Place the transfer copy face down on the fabric.
5. Transfer to fabric by heat setting with pressure. Some transfer papers require a heat press.

To use heat transfer paper efficiently, group several photos or enlarge smaller ones to take full advantage of the sheet size, then copy your images.

Transfer sheets are designed for use in a hydraulic heat press, like those used to print T-shirts, and require both high heat and intense pressure. Some fiber artists now have their own presses—dry mount, Elna, or heat transfer presses. Without a press, it is important to become a human heat press by leaning very heavily on your iron. A firm surface under the iron works better than a heavily padded one. Use an old iron with no steam vents.

Do not use steam to heat set. Allow about 30 seconds with your iron at the highest temperature the fabric will tolerate (optimum temperature for transfer is 350° to 375°F). Use both hands and lean into the iron to get maximum pressure.

Peel the paper away while it is still hot, starting at one corner and using a single steady motion. An uneven pull may result in color breaks. If the paper is hard to separate, continue heating; it must be separated while hot. If your photo is not transferring well, you are probably applying inadequate heat or pressure. Practice helps, but successful transfers are not difficult. Copy shops, T-shirt shops, or specialty transfer companies use heavy-duty presses, which help to avoid any mottling or breaking of the image. There are also mail-order companies which specialize in transferring your photo to cloth. See Source List on page 24.

It is less expensive when you supply your own transfer sheets, but they must be compatible with the specific machine you are using. Different papers have been formulated for different machines. Many shops will work only with their own papers, so confirm that a shop will print on your paper before you invest. Canon, for example, will not warranty their machines if any paper other than the one they provide is used. Paper made for the color laser copier will not work in a laser or inkjet printer.

Color laser copier transfers work best on white or light fabrics, since open areas of a copy let fabric color show. G&S carries a product called PAROopaque™, developed for printing on black or dark colors. The disadvantage of this product is that it gives a somewhat plastic, almost rubbery surface. While not preferable for quilts or garments, it would have some application for wall pieces.

TROUBLESHOOTING FOR HEAT TRANSFER SHEETS

Problem: Image has not adhered or is incomplete.

Solution: Apply more heat, more pressure, or use a fresher copy.

                 Use a fabric free of finishes.

Problem: There is a line through the print.

Solution: Remove the paper with a single steady pull.

Louise Thompson
Pleasure Ladies, 60" x 80"
photo: Ferrari Color

Louise heat transferred images of the five smoking ladies to background fabric, using a hot iron. Additional figures were transferred to various colored cloths and then appliquéd to the panel. The background fabric was spritzed with dye, and circles of netting were used to suggest pale suns. The lower border was "rag painted," a technique in which Louise substituted a cloth for a brush, and dabbed on the paint. Other borders were marbleized and hand-dyed. Branches, fish, kelp, and flowers were all appliquéd.

Jennifer Angus
Transmigration Series: Suchart as Native American of the Southwest
48" x 36"
photo: Thomas Moore

In her *Transmigration Series,* Jennifer explores issues of culture clash—whether of herself in her husband's (Thai) culture, or of him in hers (Canadian). Enlarging the image 400 percent, Jennifer makes multi-page transfers, piecing sections together in puzzle shapes to avoid the appearance of a grid. She combines her own photographs with historical ones.

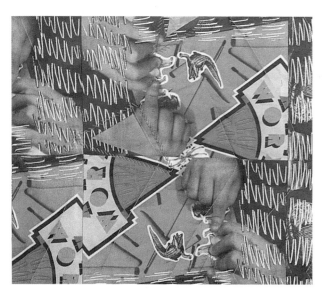

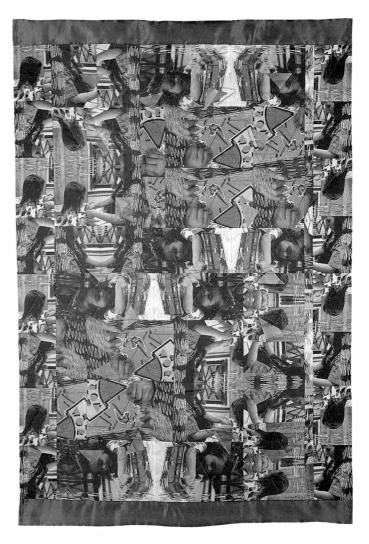

Sandra Sider
Women at Work and Play, No. 5
64" x 44"
Detail of *Women at Work and Play, No. 5*
photo: Sandra Sider

Sandra often manipulates her photos before having transfers made. On color prints she scratches through the emulsion with a scalpel or similar tool, cutting through to the paper base. The color transfer is then made of the altered photo.

Hamish Amish Quilters:
Anne Becker, Julia Biderman,
Sylvia Edelstein, Mildred Kaplan,
Eve Marsh, Ethel Rosenfeld,
Ellie Sazer, Barbara Vogel
Ellis Island Quilt, 60" x 72"
photo: Steven Jay Schwartz

Photo prints offer a visual record
and a capsule history of the
immigrant experience—a tribute
to those who came through
Ellis Island in the early 1900s.
Sepia-toned pictures from family
collections were transferred to
muslin at a local photocopy shop.
Lady Liberty and the Main
Building at Ellis, were hand-
painted with fabric paints.
Turn-of-the-century luggage carts
from a Sears catalog were
transferred along with copies of
passports for this evocative and
powerful quilt.

Gretchen Echols
*Rita Keeps on Smiling While the Blues
Are in the Basement and Her Heart
Is in the Deep Freeze*, 45" x 51½"
photo: Roger Schreiber

Using color laser copier transfer
work, Gretchen makes her
commentary on depression and
how it manifests itself in the
lives of many women—the
presentation of perfection and
beauty masking a reality of neglect
and disintegration. "Rita" is a color
laser copy from a childhood
collection of paper dolls. The house,
taken from a photo, is also a color
laser copy transfer. Postage stamps,
image cut-outs, and faces from
commercial fabrics were fused to
the panel using Wonder-Under.

Marsha Burdick
DNA, 83" x 86"
photo: Mike Shire Photography

The tumbling block pattern
used to resemble a photo cube,
includes photo transfers of five
generations of Marsha's family.
An anonymous poem, from a quilt
guild newsletter, was thermal
screened onto the border.
A representation of the double
helix **DNA** molecule is quilted
into the border, making a
comment on family heritage.

Sandra Sider
Women at Work and Play, No. 7
50" x 46"
photo: Sandra Sider

These arresting figures are
photo-transferred to fabric by
Aneta Sperber at Photo Textiles.
Sandra gives explicit directions
as to size of prints, reversals,
numbers, etc. This costs a little
more than transferring your own,
but she finds it avoids wasted or
unused prints.

Jennifer Angus
Tattooed Woman, 60" x 36"
photo: Jeremy Jones

Jennifer works with overlays of heat transfer images to create complex combinations of pattern. This language of pattern, she states, can "identify a people, a region from which they come, as well as a person's age, profession, and social status within a society." Her *Tattooed Woman* is a large piece worked on felt and embellished with beads and embroidery.

Kathleen Deneris
Olivia's Quilt, 50" x 36"
photo: Kathleen Deneris

Another fine example of the transfer used as a way of recording is seen in *Olivia's Quilt.* A drawing by a five-year-old girl was enlarged and reduced as needed, and sometimes portions were added or cut away to create this vibrant, delightful quilt. Kathleen transferred the drawings to cloth using thermal transfer paper on a color copier.

alternate ways
OF USING copiers

Color copiers use three colors of ink in addition to black: red (magenta), blue (cyan), and yellow. Any single color or combination of colors can be selected to create unusual effects. Blue and black inks, for example, yield an indigo color. Red and black produce a sepia tone.

Either full color or black and white originals can be printed in a single color for a monochromatic effect. A black overlay adds depth to a single color. Most copy shops have one specially trained employee to work with and adjust colors on the color laser copier. Even in a full-color print, the intensity of each color can be adjusted independently.

Some fiber artists prefer using their color laser copies directly with no transfer. The color copy is usually protected in some way—with clear <u>acetate</u>, transparent fabric, or an adhesive coating, which limits cleaning and washing but adds the desired image. Other artists have developed unique variations for their color copies.

Deborah Melton Anderson
Dematerialization of the Walls of Stamboul, 55" x 47"
photo: **Slide Service International**

Heat transfers combined with monoprints produced the energetic, lively patterns of this quilt. By placing her transfers over pleated, tucked, braided, and otherwise manipulated fabric, the artist created patterns of unprinted shapes which darted through the colors. Deborah prefers to do her own transfers using a heat press made specifically for T-shirts. She uses transfers no larger than the plate of her press, piecing the transfers together by moving from one to another across the whole-cloth design. Space between the edge of the press and the hinges allows for the excess fabric. Where the transfers touch, she gives special attention to how those seams work in the overall pattern, sometimes quilting on the lines to incorporate them into the design.

Gretchen Echols
Jolly Dolly Dingle, 48" x 72"
Detail of *Jolly Dolly Dingle*
photo: William Wickett

Gretchen's paper dolls, color copied onto plain paper, not heat transfer paper, were covered with a protective coat. She used flexible, lightweight Mylar and therefore prefers rolling the panel to folding it. Words printed with alphabet stamps and fabric paint float on bright colored patches of fabric in the borders. This delightful quilted textile allows Dolly Dingle to peer, unperturbed, from a colorful array of patterns and plaids.

Joan Tobin
Pillow, 11" x 16"

Joan used a color laser copier heat transfer (printed in black only) for the figures in the far right of the pillow, while the images at center and on the left were silk-screen printed from the same image.

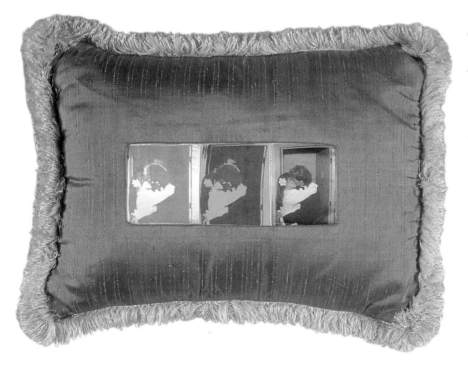

heat transfer spray

SOURCE LIST

LaserTrans 4000 Transfer Spray, 37

A new product for the transfer of color or black and white laser prints is a spray-on material designed to be used with a heat press. While one container costs almost $50.00, it will cover approximately one-hundred 8$\frac{1}{2}$" x 11" sheets. The transfer spray works with cotton or cotton/poly blend, and is washfast, though it is not designed for inkjet printers. The transfer spray, developed in Spain, is available at some copy or T-shirt shops, and the company told me it would set up individual accounts.

solvent and medium transfers
FOR color laser copiers

The processes for solvent and medium transfers of color are identical to those for black and white. These are described in detailed step-by-step instructions found on pages 15 and 17.

Color-copied photos can be transferred individually to fabric, or they can first be collaged and all transferred in one step. Double thicknesses of paper are not as easily penetrated by solvent as a single thickness. Therefore, it may be necessary to make a new color copy of a collage in order to transfer it successfully.

Patricia Malarcher
Silk City Album, 9" x 9"
photo: D. James Dee

In *Silk City Album* Patricia made a very different use of the color laser copier transfers. After her image was printed onto the transfer paper she heat set it to a reflective Mylar. Even with a protective cloth as a buffer, it was difficult to determine the exact time at which the transfer was complete, before the Mylar melted. To assemble the panel, Patricia used nine squares of reflective Mylar over which smaller squares of silk were placed. These were topped in turn by her transferred pieces. All squares were machine sewn, leaving threads to create a linear tangle to contrast with the grid of the panel. The title relates to Patterson, NJ, once known as **Silk City** because of its many silk mills.

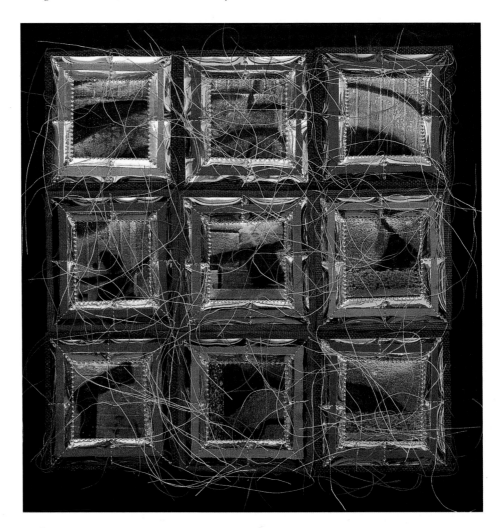

printers

Computer printers have quietly edged their way into fiber artists' studios. With the printer tucked between the serger and the cutting board, the possibilities for using lettering, scanned photographs, and original drawings have expanded immensely. We now have the enticing attraction of printing in full color onto cloth, eliminating the transfer process entirely.

This chapter includes techniques for using laser printers, inkjet printers, dot matrix printers, and typewriters.

Most inkjet printers use water-based, rather than alcohol-based inks. The water-based inks are not permanent on fabric unless used with transfer sheets made specifically for inkjet printers.

While all copiers use heat, not all printers do. Laser printers (which deposit toner) use heat—inkjet printers do not. Some transfer papers require heat—others cannot tolerate heat. A transfer paper for the color laser copier can go through the inkjet printer (without harming the machine), but the ink will just sit on the surface of the paper and will not transfer. A low-heat transfer paper cannot tolerate the high heat of a copier or laser printer. Products and machines must be compatible. Always read directions that come with transfers.

Note: A distinction is made in this chapter between laser printers and inkjet printers. The Bubble Jet® (Canon), DeskJet® (HP), Apple®, Epson®, and all other inkjets come under our general term of inkjet printers. This chapter includes:

laser printers

inkjet printers

dot matrix printer, transfer ribbon

typewriter, direct printing

LASER PRINTERS

Laser printers deposit toner on paper with heat, like copiers. The primary advantages for their use by fiber artists are: 1) the intensity of the black can be controlled through the computer's print dialogue box; and 2) the artist has the ability to scan in original images or use computer art and fonts. Scanners are machines that read or "scan" an image and then store it in your computer. Some scanners will scan transparencies and slides as well as text or line art. They vary in terms of the image size they will scan. Scanning photos gobbles up computer memory at an alarming rate, and glitches inevitably occur. The more you know about your computer, the better you will be able to control your files, expand your design options, and reduce the possibility of crashes.

Most laser printouts on paper can be solvent transferred to cloth using the same method described in Solvent Transfer on page 17. To avoid the use of solvents, just run the fabric directly through the printer.

running fabric THROUGH the laser printer

For this process the fabric needs to be stabilized or stiffened. Read the precautions and directions given in Chapter 1, Running Fabric Through the Copier, on pages 9 and 10.

WHAT YOU NEED	THE PROCESS
Stabilized fabric	1. Place stabilized fabric in the printer tray (adjusting printer to accept heavy stock).
Laser printer	2. Print the image.
Image or lettering	3. Dry thoroughly. Remove stabilizer backing, if used.
Tissue paper	4. Cover image with tissue paper. Heat set.
Iron and board	5. Test for washability.

A gentle, light rinsing removes almost no toner, though large areas of black may lighten. The toner will be partially removed or lightened with vigorous scrubbing action or an abrasive soap. If your print does not fare well in the washability test, there are several ways to enhance the permanence of the print: 1) more heat setting, 2) spray fixatives, and 3) transfer finishes.

The washability of laser prints is determined by several factors including the temperature at which the toner is deposited. This will vary from one machine to the next, or from one brand to another. Experiment. Since fabric and thread finishes may prevent toner from being absorbed, prewash fabric using Synthrapol™, or use PFP fabric. Both time and heat help to assure permanence.

Heat Setting

Use a hot iron and a firm, padded ironing surface. Dry the print overnight. Cover the printed area with tissue to prevent toner from sticking to the iron. Press for one to two minutes. Some designers use Silicone or Teflon® pressing cloths, and a few find that a water spray before <u>heat setting</u> is helpful. If you have a heat press, press at 350°F for 10 seconds, increasing time if needed.

Spray Fixative

If heat does not set your print, give it two or three coats of clear spray (Krylon Workable Fixatif®, for example). Dry each coat thoroughly (an hour or more) before adding another. As some prints may run, start with a very light misting. A final water rinse will restore some of the softness and pliability.

Transfer Finishes

Transfer sheets made for the inkjet or color laser copier can be ironed over the laser transfer to provide a protective coating. All stiffen the fabric somewhat, but after several heat settings the transfers seem to soak into the fabric, making it softer. Mending tape works the same way. Iron the tape over the laser transfer, then peel off the backing fabric, leaving a thin protective film over the print.

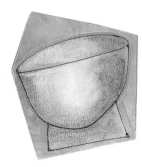

TROUBLESHOOTING FOR RUNNING FABRIC THROUGH THE LASER PRINTER

Problem: Most of the image washed out of the fabric.

Solution: Use PFP fabric.

Use higher heat or a heat press.

Try fixative or transfer finishes.

Try a different printer.

Problem: Printer will not accept the fabric/freezer-paper sandwich.

Solution: Use a lighter weight fabric (organdy or silk).

Adjust the paper thickness setting on the printer.

Joan Schulze
Detail of *Water Music*, full quilt on page 16.

Lettering used by Joan was scanned into her computer. She printed directly on cloth by running the stabilized fabric through her laser printer.

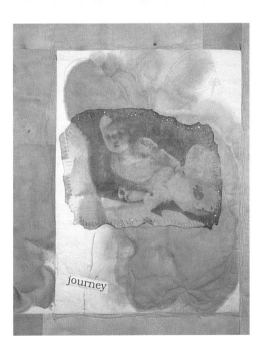

Darcy Falk
Journey, 21" x 16"
photo: Michael Falk

Darcy scanned a photo into her computer so it could be laser printed directly onto silk organza. The organza was first ironed onto freezer paper, and after printing, was allowed to dry for 24 hours. The image was then set with a medium hot iron. Acrylic wash painting along with layering, burning, and stitching completed the piece.

Gerry Chase
Hands Down, First Edition
47" x 60"
photo: Roger Schreiber

Gerry's interest in text, and its ability to affect one's visual experience, prompted the design of *Hands Down, First Edition*. The historic use of quilts as vehicles for messages is reflected in this work, in which the visual message is dominant. She selected excerpts from magazines, scanned them into the computer, and enlarged them from two to five inches. After printing them on stabilized fabric in the black and white laser printer, she cut out the letters and bonded them to fusible fabric. These strips were then pieced or zigzag stitched to hand-dyed fabrics, and pastels were used to cover the white areas surrounding the letters. After spraying with fixative, she added other hand-painted details.

Gerry Chase
Nine-Patch II: Cups, 25" x 24"
photo: Roger Schreiber

After making her drawings on fabric using ink in a tjanting tool, Gerry scanned the image into her computer. She printed images onto stabilized fabric in her laser printer. Over these black and white images she established values with Pentel® fabric crayons, then layed in light washes of color with acrylic paint (Liquitex® or Golden). She added further painting to get the effect she wanted, avoiding any thick layers of acrylic (at which the sewing machine balks). At the lower edge of the panel a hand-carved stamp was used to create the vertical lines. Her twin themes of "exaltation of the ordinary" and "the power of repetition" are both clearly evident in this compelling piece.

transfer prints
ON THE laser printer

Special heat transfer toners (BlackLightning®) can be purchased for the laser printer. The printouts on paper can be heat transferred to any fabric with 50% or more synthetic fiber content. For BlackLightning the recommended heat press temperature is 400°F for 30 seconds. For a dry iron with no steam vents, use the highest setting for one minute. Several transfers can be made from one print.

The special transfer toners for the laser printer contain sublimation dyes which are permanent and colorfast on synthetics. To use cotton or a blend of less than 50% synthetic, use Laser Trans 4000, a spray which can be applied to make the fabrics more receptive to the sublimation (disperse) dye. After heat transferring they will be permanent on cottons or blends.

A transfer toner must be purchased for each color, and the colors are printed on paper one at a time. Using a graphics program with a color separation capability, you can print a paper several times, each time in a different color. All colors can then be heat transferred to fabric with one step. Printing two or three colors, each from a separate transfer paper, is problematic because of <u>registration</u>. Fabrics shift and visual alignment is difficult.

While initial cost of the toner is high ($140), hundreds of transfer sheets can be made from a single cartridge. The finished work can be washed in hot water with bleach and the image will not wash out.

SOURCE LIST

Heat Transfer Toner
(BlackLightning), 12

Laser Trans 4000 Transfer Spray, 37

TROUBLESHOOTING FOR TRANSFER PRINTS ON THE LASER PRINTER

Problem: Prints are pale.

Solution: Select a design with heavier, stronger lines.

Set printer option to bold or dense.

Use more heat, as much as the synthetic fabric will tolerate.

Problem: A double image appears.

Solution: Use clean paper, clean cover on ironing surface.

Do not let fabric or paper shift.

Problem: Paper won't peel off the fabric.

Solution: Peel when hot, or let cool completely. The transfer is "tacky" when warm.

Bonnie Meltzer
Detail of scarf

For her scarf, Bonnie scanned leaves into the computer, reduced them, and again printed on paper with BlackLightning in black and magenta. The print was heat transferred to cloth. Subsequent transfers from the same print got lighter and lighter, creating a range of intensities.

Rose Ann Dayton
Detail of *Rose Ann's Scarf*

This scarf was transferred from
a computer drawing by Rose Ann,
a fourth grader in Bonnie
Meltzer's class.

Bonnie Meltzer
Detail of teaching bandana,
Mistakes and How to Fix Them

Bonnie uses BlackLightning's Iron-
on Laser Printer Transfer Toners,
working in magenta and black
only. Magenta produces additional
hues when it is transferred over
colored fabrics. Over yellow fabric, for example, a red results.
Bonnie also paints directly on the
paper prints with liquid disperse
dyes, giving her a full range of colors. As the print is heat transferred to fabric, so is the disperse
dye. Bonnie's teaching bandana
contains computer lettering and
computer-drawn figures.
Additional color was applied
with dye markers and Deka®
Fabric Paints.

laser prints with foil

SOURCE LIST

Ad Maze, 3, 8

Jones Tones® Foils, 3, 28

other foils, 3, 34

Ritva

This example shows Ritva's
ubiquitous portrait, printed with
toner on cloth and foiled by heat
setting with an iron. I have also
screen-printed foil adhesive
directly onto cloth, then foiled it,
with beautiful results.

Various metallic foils are available on the market in brilliant reflective colors with dull backing. These thin foils are actually Mylar-coated papers and are made to be burnished or heat set to an adhesive made especially for their use. This adhesive (Aleene's 3-D Foiling Glue™, for example) can be painted, stamped, silk-screened, printed, or block-printed onto fabric. The foil adds a brilliant and reflective surface. Since foils were developed for paper, smooth fabrics will be more reflective than textured fabrics.

Since some foils adhere to toner with heat setting, almost anything that can be copied or printed with toner can also be foiled. A laser copy can be covered with foil (metallic side up), then with tissue, and heat set. When the foiling sheet is removed the reflective layer remains. This requires experimenting, as cloth is more difficult to foil than paper.

Here is a nifty method of applying the heat-set foil using the laser printer. Print your image or letters onto <u>stabilized</u> fabric. Then re-run the fabric through the printer covered by a sheet of foil but without printing it. Heat will set foil to toner, and the excess foil will peel off. Theoretically. My laser printer is new, and perhaps the "improved" toners do not bond to the foil. It is essential to use foil that is transferred by heat setting, not burnishing.

TROUBLESHOOTING FOR LASER PRINTS WITH FOIL

Problem: You cannot get the foil to transfer.
Solution: Use a foil made for this purpose.
             Adjust the page-thickness control for better contact.
Problem: Only part of the image accepted the foil.
Solution: Reposition foil and heat set again using more pressure.
             Use a more dense print; toner may be too light.

INKJET PRINTERS

Since most inkjet printers use water-soluble rather than alcohol-based inks, they are non-permanent (ever sneeze on an inkjet print?). If you have already run silk or cotton through your inkjet printer you probably saw those gorgeous colors flow down the drain as the fabric was rinsed. Textile artists have tried to arrest the escaping, fugitive colors in various ways, but have had limited success. So, until jet printers have permanent inks, here are some alternatives.

spray finishes AND transfer

Spraying a fixative over an inkjet print will help set or fix the color on the fabric. Among the brands preferred by fiber artists are Retayne and Krylon Clear. These measures help, but do not entirely solve the problem. The hand of the fabric is changed, leaving it a little less soft and flexible.

A major concern with spray finishes is the potential harm from vapors. Spray out of doors or with good ventilation and a paper mask (such as painters use). Use special caution if you make extensive or continuous use of the fixatives.

Another method of making the jet prints more permanent involves the use of transfers (Canon TR-101) to seal or fix the ink to the fabric. After printing the image on the fabric, heat set it. An unprinted sheet of inkjet transfer paper, cut to cover the image, is placed with green lines up and with polymer side face-to-face with the image. It is heat transferred, then rinsed in a dilute vinegar solution. The polymer serves as a fixative which coats the fabric and gives it a damp look, a slight sheen, and permanency.

Mending tape, applied in the same way, gives similar results. The mending tape is heat set to the image and peeled away while it is still hot. Should it be necessary to overlap the mending tape, overlapping edges will not show.

Heat transfer paper (made for color laser copiers) did not work well, as some of the color washed out. However, Becky Sundquist found that if she heat set the color laser copier transfer paper several times and used a Teflon pressing cloth, the transparent coating seemed to soak into the cloth, adding permanence and pliability.

TROUBLESHOOTING FOR SPRAY FINISHES AND TRANSFER

Problem: Colors faded when the fixative-coated cloth was washed.

Solution: Use a heavier spray or additional coats.

            Try mending tape or transfer paper as a sealer.

Problem: Transfer sheet stiffens the fabric.

Solution: Heat set it several times until transfer "soaks" into fabric.

Problem: Mending tape didn't peel off the inkjet printed fabric.

Solution: Re-heat the tape and remove it while it's hot.

The following quilts make complex use of computers and printers. The artists know the effects they want, and by careful manipulation achieve the desired results. Thorough familiarity with the computer is essential; the drawing and graphics programs they use are sophisticated and sensitive, and require knowledge and experience to operate.

SOURCE LIST

Canon TR-101®, 2, 6, 26

Krylon Clear, 1, 3, 22, 34

Mending tape, 4

Retayne™, 21

Ritva

Printed on an inkjet printer, this image was then covered with Canon TR-101 to "fix" it.

Becky Sundquist
Arctic Light, 37¹/₂" x 30¹/₂"
photo: Carina Woolrich

Becky scanned three original photographs of trees into her computer, then manipulated, rearranged and altered the sizes and colors. Additional scanned photos of sky, water and foliage were developed into the design on a **CAD** program to create a full size grid pattern, printing the twenty page mock-up on her inkjet printer. She adhered it to foamcore, and cut templates for her fabric. Freezer paper backed fabrics were printed in light, medium, and dark values to achieve variations needed for the streaks of sunlight. Background areas (sky, lake, leaves) were printed first. All printed fabrics were sprayed with Krylon brand fixative, dried, then embellished with chalk, colored pencils and watercolors (anything at hand!). After removing the freezer paper, she soaked the fabric in Synthrapol and rinsed it in Mil-soft®. Her composition required constant shifting between printer and appliqué. Her printed tree forms were appliquéd over background areas so that sky showed through. **Becky is fearless in her use of the printer, running collaged fabrics and heavy textures through on the setting for envelopes.** After scanning in real birch bark, Becky simplified its design to eliminate obvious repeats and printed the border on "crinkle silk."

Caryl Bryer Fallert
Mother's Day, 20" x 22"
photo: Caryl Bryer Fallert

Caryl's quilt, a tribute to her mother, utilized the copier, computer, and printer. She scanned in a collection of portraits of her female ancestors (the earliest, 1791). Each photo was transformed to echo the nineteenth-century oval mats with larger ovals reserved for pictures of her mother. The last photograph of her mother holding a grand-niece was scanned in and enlarged to fill one side of the quilt. Once printed out full size, a paper pattern for appliqué templates was made. The hands and face were photocopied directly on light-colored fabric and enhanced with Prismacolor pencils. Other parts of the figure were appliquéd and machine embroidered. The photos were laser-printed onto paper, then photocopied onto white fabric which had been fused to Wonder-Under. The images were heat set and fused to the surface of the quilt. The words, spiraling through the center, were added with permanent marker.

canon fabric sheets FS-101
DESIGNED FOR CANON BUBBLE JET COMPUTER PRINTERS

This is a computer-ready package consisting of a piece of white fabric attached by lines of adhesive to a transparent backing. It is designed for printing with the Canon Bubble Jet printer directly onto fabric.

The strips of adhesive on the fabric sheet align with the feeders in Canon printers, but when used in the Hewlett-Packard and Stylewriter 2400® printers, the strips caused the fabric to be pulled from the backing, rendering a misprint. I reapplied the cloth to freezer paper and had great results. Since there is no heat generated in the inkjet printers, neither adhesives nor plastics pose a problem. Even when Canon's "Colorfast" rinse step was eliminated, the image was vibrant and seemed brighter than when the fixative was used. It did not fade in hand-washing. The colorfast fixative is designed to make colors less subject to fading.

WHAT YOU NEED
Scanned image or computer art work
Canon Fabric Sheet FS-101
Inkjet printer
Iron and board

THE PROCESS
1. Place Canon Fabric Sheet in printer tray.
2. Print the image.
3. Peel fabric from backing.
4. Rinse in Canon's Colorfast solution, following the directions.
5. Cover with paper, and press.

SOURCE LIST
Canon FS-101®, 6

After printing on your fabric sheet, simply peel the fabric from the transparent backing. A packet of Colorfast (provided with the fabric sheet) is used for the rinse, then the print is dried and ironed. Results are permanent and vibrant.

TROUBLESHOOTING FOR CANON FABRIC SHEETS
Problem: Fabric sheet doesn't feed through printer correctly.
Solution: Eliminate the clear backing sheet and stabilize the fabric with freezer paper.
Problem: Spots or specks appear on the print.
Solution: Clean all copy surfaces so they are free of lint, threads, and dust.

Ann Johnston
Merry-go-round 2, 58" x 71"
photo: Reprinted with the express written consent of Canon Computer Systems, Inc. All rights reserved.

Ann scanned her collection of carousel photographs onto Photo **CD ROM** (at a local copy shop) at five different resolutions. Using Adobe Photoshop® she then adjusted colors and (using the rubber stamp tool) cloned background over unwanted parts (such as poles that cut through the horses). The huge files (48,000 Kilobytes for just one crown) were subdivided into three files, from which she could print and paint. She sketched her plan, arranged it on the computer and saved it in separate layers. The overall composition, in 7" x 8" images, was printed on ten-to-the-inch blue line graph paper, which resisted the inkjet print to create a clear grid pattern. Each grid, enlarged to full scale with the high resolution doubled, was printed onto a 9¹/₂" x 14" Canon Fabric Sheet with a Canon BJC 4100 printer. Overlap at the edges assisted in alignment for piecing. To avoid grid seams, horse parts (mane, harness, head) were printed separately, put onto fusible backing and laid in place. To prevent colors from showing through the white areas, she cut away background prints, leaving cut edges butted together perfectly. Rhinestones added sparkle to the satin-stitched join lines. The zebra required two prints, with several more for the background panel. After this very involved assembly, Ann added quilting to echo the carousel figures.

Judy Mathieson
Autumn in New England, 65" x 65"
photo: Reprinted with the express written consent of Canon Computer Systems, Inc. All rights reserved.

Autumn in New England is a computer-generated quilt based on photos from a *Corel Stock Photo Two* library of royalty-free images on CD. Using a scanned photo of Judy's *Attic Windows* design from an earlier quilt, Judy's husband Jack produced a mock-up on the computer with images inserted in the open areas of the grid. Each print had an allowance for seams. Each of the larger corner "windows," for example, was made up of four prints. Wood textures were printed in varying values to create effects of light and shadow. All prints were made on Canon Fabric Sheets. Judy machine quilted the piece by outlining the windows and using a diagonal over the landscape.

Sharyn Craig
A Father's Life, 71" x 72"
photo: Reprinted with the express written consent of Canon Computer Systems, Inc. All rights reserved.

All the fabrics in this quilt are printed on 9½" x 14" Canon Fabric Sheets, giving Sharyn an impression of being "grandma on the prairie," limited to small pieces of fabric. Using public-domain compact disk images, Sharyn selected carpeting, leather, fabric, granite, and marbleized patterns in black and white. She added scanned sepia photos of her father, and enhanced them by adding a subtle color range. After printing over a hundred different pieces of cloth, she pieced, assembled, and quilted the work.

transfer sheets FOR inkjet printers

Inkjet transfers are special polymer-treated papers which, when run through an inkjet printer, can be heat transferred to cloth. Manufactured as T-shirt transfers, the instructions list the specific printers for which they are designed. While the TR-101 was made specifically for Canon printers, it works in other inkjet printers as well. I have had excellent results with a Hewlett-Packard printer and a Stylewriter 2400. It is important to know that this paper is designed for use with water-based inks.

SOURCE LIST

Affinity's High Definition Inkjet
Print Media, 20

Canon TR-101, 2, 6, 26

Hanes T-Shirt Transfer Paper™, 26

Jet-Ware!®, 27

WHAT YOU NEED

Inkjet printer

Scanned image or computer
artwork

Transfer sheet for inkjet printer

White distilled vinegar

Iron and board

THE PROCESS

1. Place only one sheet of transfer paper in the printer tray.
2. Print image.
3. Trim away any excess paper, leaving only the image.
4. Use a vinegar rinse for the fabric (one cup white distilled vinegar and a low-level washer full of cold water). Dry fabric.
5. Preheat fabric to remove any moisture.
6. Place inkjet color print face down on fabric (green lines up or showing).
7. Heat set. Use a hand iron on a hard ironing surface, such as Formica® or Masonite®. A heat press is recommended.

To maximize color retention for all brands listed, put vinegar in washer and add water to low level. Add unprinted fabric. Then complete wash cycle with cold water. Remove fabric immediately and dry under normal settings. The fabric is now ready for transfer.

To print a photo onto a transfer sheet, you will need to scan the photo into the computer. If you don't have a scanner, some print shops will scan your photo and copy it to a disk. Make sure you have compatible software to open the file. Thousands of clip-art images are also available for immediate use.

Transfer sheets must be compatible with the specific printer you are using. Those for the color laser copier repel the water-based inks. The TR-101 for inkjet printers will not work for the color laser copier. Neither one can be used in a black and white laser printer.

Hanes has T-shirt Maker software (which requires Windows® 3.1 or Windows® '95) with ready-to-print graphics. But they also sell their T-shirt transfer paper by the packet. It can be printed in the inkjet printer for transfer to cloth with an iron.

Some computer printers require that sheets be inverted for printing—others accept them face up. The Canon TR-101, Jet-Ware!, and Affinity's High Definition InkJet Print Media are all fabric transfer papers printed with green lines to identify the back of the page. Since this is a one-step process, the image will be reversed. If your computer has mirror-image capability, use that to correct the transfer. The transfers on fabric will be slightly tacky until they are dry, so avoid stacking them. Wash fabric prints in cold water, detergent with color protection, and no bleach. Do not iron directly on the transfer.

TROUBLESHOOTING FOR TRANSFER SHEETS FOR INKJET PRINTERS

Problem: Transfer is blurred or double.
Solution: Stabilize fabric, especially on a T-shirt.
Problem: Prints are crazed or spotty.
Solution: Use higher heat and more pressure, holding the iron in each spot for about 15 seconds.

Shirley Grace
Something's Fishy, 29" x 30"

Shirley scanned one of my paper collages into her computer and manipulated the colors to produce a warm and subdued color range. Prints were made on TR-101 paper with an inkjet printer. Excess paper was trimmed, leaving only the fish. It was transferred to a cotton/poly blend, assembled, and quilted.

Gretchen Echols
Bob and Rita Try to Forget
48" x 96"
photo: William Wickett

Color copies from the artist's childhood paper doll collection provide a focus for her musings. Gretchen worked with a color scanner to copy her paper doll images into the computer. She then ran her fabric through a color jet printer, and the resulting image was fused using Wonder-Under to the background fabric. The forks and spoons, which form a halo, were cut from novelty fabric and fused to the fabric. Ribbons, buttons, and found objects complete the picture.

DOT MATRIX PRINTER, TRANSFER RIBBON

Special heat-transfer ribbons allow you to transfer single colors to fabric from dot matrix printouts. The ribbons are saturated with disperse dye and yield their color with heat (see Chapter 4). They will yield the brightest transfer and provide the greatest permanence when heat set to synthetic fabrics.

SOURCE LIST

Heat-transfer ribbon, 17, 18

WHAT YOU NEED

A computer with graphics capabilities (unless you are doing text only)

Dot matrix impact printer

Heat-transfer ribbons

Fabric (at least 50% synthetic) in light or bright colors

Iron and board

THE PROCESS

1. Produce your original image or lettering using your computer.
2. Set computer for mirror-image, if possible, necessary, or desirable.
3. Turn printer off. Replace standard ribbon with a heat-transfer ribbon.
4. Print a copy of your image on paper.
5. Cover and protect the ironing board.
6. Place the fabric right side up on board.
7. Place the print face side down on the fabric. Cover with paper to avoid scorching your fabric.
8. Heat set with a dry hot iron for 30 seconds.

Transfers on 100% cotton are less vivid and less permanent than those on synthetics. Fabrics must be able to withstand the heat setting.

Your heat-transfer copy can be made on standard print paper, but you may get a better transfer with a 16-pound erasable bond. Remove the ribbon when you have finished, and do not use it for normal printing (particles in the ink can wear out the print head). Store it in a resealable plastic bag.

TROUBLESHOOTING FOR DOT MATRIX PRINTER, TRANSFER RIBBON

Problem: The prints are unclear or double.

Solution: Adjust the paper thickness lever. (Page must be held firmly in place to avoid an echo print.)

Problem: Prints are light or pale.

Solution: Select a print mode that deposits more ink ("best" rather than "draft" copy, or adjust density in the printing option.)

Use a new ribbon.

Use synthetic fabric or a hotter iron.

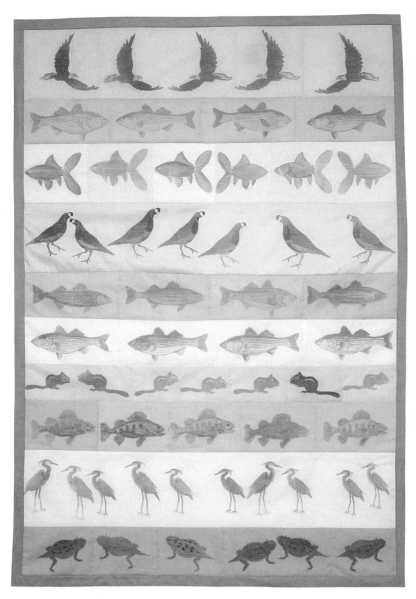

Susan L. Smeltzer
Fish and Friends, 58" x 45"

Computer clip art was the source for the fish, birds, and animals in Susan's *Fish and Friends*. She substituted a black heat-transfer ribbon for the standard ribbon in her dot matrix printer. After filling a page with images and reversing some of them so that the fish could swim both east and west, she printed out several pages. She colored the prints with Crayola Craft Fabric Crayons™, cut the prints apart, and heat transferred them individually.

Five Women, 11" x 15"

Using Microsoft Word® with a built-in drawing program, I drew the figure, repeated, overlapped, and printed it with black heat-transfer ribbon in the dot matrix printer. The printed paper was trimmed and heat set to stabilized synthetic fabric. I added color to the figures with Marvy® paint-tip markers.

TYPEWRITER, DIRECT PRINTING

Run fabric through the typewriter and you can put messages, letters, or your entire family history on the back of a quilt. For permanence, purchase an indelible ribbon. Heat set the typing after it dries (allow a couple of hours) and it will withstand washing. If you use a standard ribbon, dry and heat set the typed message, then test in cool water with mild liquid detergent. Some standard ribbons give permanent results, others last through several washings, and a few wash out completely and immediately. Test yours, and remember that fiber content and fabric treatments affect permanence. General Ribbon Corp., a major supplier of typewriter ribbons, considers all their ribbons to be fairly permanent, though they acknowledge the type will eventually wash out of fabric. After heat setting, spray typed fabric with Krylon Workable Fixatif, made for use on rag papers to make it more permanent.

Stiffened fabric is easier to roll into the machine than limp fabric. Use any of the methods described in Chapter 1 on pages 9-11, though overall lamination is less crucial for this method. A few fabrics (such as glazed cotton) will roll into the machine with no additional stiffening at all. The smoother the weave of the cloth, the clearer the message.

WHAT YOU NEED

Standard ribbon or indelible ribbon

PFP fabric (smooth and slightly crisp or laminated)

Typewriter

Iron and board

Optional:
Krylon Workable Fixitif

THE PROCESS

1. Roll stiffened fabric into the typewriter.
2. Type your message.
3. Remove backing, if any, cover the print with tissue, and heat set.
4. Test for permanence.
5. Spray with Krylon Workable Fixatif if necessary for greater permanence.

A typewritten cloth letter in a cloth envelope is a great way of attaching a detailed history to the back of a quilt. The typewritten letter can be removed for washing.

Patricia Kennedy-Zafred
Shot from the Back, 22" x 16³/₄"
Detail of *Shot from the Back*
photo: Peter Sheffler

Patricia ran her fabrics directly through a daisy wheel typewriter. To create her images, the artist photocopied her own photographs onto acetate, then traced her image onto white fabric to identify the area in which she could add her typewritten messages. With messages in place, she cut out the white fabric shape, placed it on the red fabric, and layered the acetate on top. Machine stitching added linear patterns and quilted the layers. The torn proof sheet is also stitched into the composition.

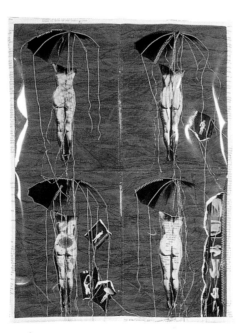

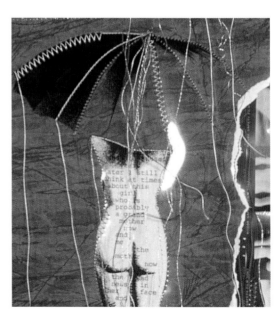

drawing & painting

A fresh box of crayons prismatically aligned with sharpened points and wrappers intact is nearly irresistible. Inexpensive and bright, both crayons and dye sticks offer great ways to add colorful drawings to cloth. Furthermore, no studio is complete without an assortment of marking pens of all sizes, chalks, dye sticks, and a variety of paints. The simple, often-overlooked, humble "everyday" methods in this chapter present wonderful possibilities. They can transform fabric without any expensive equipment or materials, and require little technical knowledge. This chapter includes the techniques for using the following items:

crayons

dye sticks

markers

transfer papers

paints

C R A Y O N S

My first experience with crayon on fabric was in third grade, with plain old crayons (before the special ones for fabric). I colored the knees of my drab, oatmeal-colored, long cotton stockings. Green and violet shapes animated my knees for months and survived (to my mother's dismay) all washings. But I observed a more dramatic use of crayons when my mother took down the monks' cloth dining room draperies and penciled in an abundance of flowers and leaves. Then, with two Turkish towels in her lap, she held the iron between her knees (sole plate up), put the cloth over the iron, and colored in the designs. As the crayons heated, they melted onto the cloth, making brilliant, opaque areas of color. An old cigar box filled with broken crayon stubs had been the means of this metamorphosis which, it seemed to me, was nothing short of divine inspiration.

crayon transfer

Transfer crayons are made to be used on paper and transferred by heat to fabric. Available in brilliant hues, these disperse (sublimation) dyes in a wax base are safe for children to use. Drawings are easily transferred from paper to cloth. Used directly on cloth a smooth blending of color is more difficult to achieve, and the crayons may fume or give off excess color.

SOURCE LIST

Crayola Craft Fabric Crayons, 1, 3, 7, 34

Crayola Transfer Fabric Crayons™, 1, 3, 7

Dritz® Fabric Crayons, 1, 3, 4, 34

WHAT YOU NEED

Crayola Transfer Fabric Crayons

Paper

Fabric (65% synthetic or more, 100% is best)

Iron and board

Newsprint, or other scrap paper

THE PROCESS

1. Draw with firm strokes on bond or typing paper (not a slick paper). Shake crayon crumbs from the paper, or use masking tape to pick them up.
2. Cut fabric larger than the drawing.
3. Protect an ironing surface with paper. Place fabric right side up, with drawing on top, crayon side down. Cover with scrap paper.
4. Heat iron to highest setting the fabric will tolerate without scorching. Step-press by lifting the iron up and down firmly. Do not slide the iron. Heat until the drawing begins to show through the top sheet of paper. Children need adult supervision for this step of the transfer.

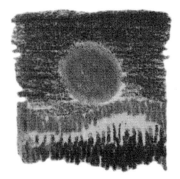

The transferred drawing will be a mirror image of the original. A second transfer will be less bright than the first. The original drawing can be re-colored to make additional prints. Insert several layers of paper inside a garment to prevent color from bleeding through. Test for washability before launching on any major project. The heat-set pieces may be washed with warm water and gentle action. Do not bleach, and never place in the dryer.

Fabric crayons can be used in another very interesting way that appeals to people who think they can't draw. Start with a black and white copy of a print or illustration, and color over it. When heat set to fabric the color drawing will transfer without the copy.

TROUBLESHOOTING FOR CRAYON TRANSFER

Problem: The image is blurred or smeared.

Solution: Secure fabric so it doesn't move.

Do not over iron.

Problem: Unwanted colors appear in the background.

Solution: Pick up all crayon crumbs before pressing, or add more crumbs and use them as texture.

Landscapes

The six small landscapes were drawn on paper with Crayola Craft Fabric Crayons and transferred to a synthetic blend fabric by heat setting. Some were transferred twice using the same original.

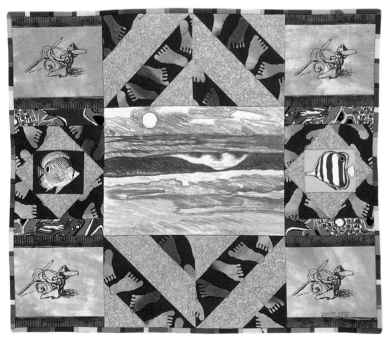

Frances R. MacEachren
Kitty Hawk Beach, 27" x 32"
Detail of *Kitty Hawk Beach*
photo: Jon Sheckler

Frances took a photograph of Kitty Hawk Beach, then made a sketch from it on paper using Dritz Fabric Crayons. The drawing was transferred to poly/cotton with a hot iron to make it permanent. Thermo-Fax® screening was used for the corner blocks of shells and vertebrae.

rubbings: direct, indirect, AND others

A rubbing is an impression or print made over a relief pattern or textured surface. Fabric stretched over texture and rubbed with crayon or pencil will reveal the pattern beneath it. Rubbings can be made direct (right on the cloth) or indirect (on paper to be transferred to cloth). The artist's term frottage, meaning to rub, refers to any pattern or design which is "lifted" or duplicated by this method.

On a very large scale, manhole covers make a great surface for rubbings. Commemorative plaques, brass plates, cornerstones, and incised letters all lend themselves to this process. Rubbings make it possible to collect things which are unmovable, unavailable, or of historical significance.

Direct Rubbings

All kinds of familiar objects can be used for crayon rubbings, though larger surfaces are more difficult to work with. Cookie boards, embossed designs on dishes or paper, filigree work, coins, tombstones, tiles, etc., are good beginning projects. Direct rubbings are preferable if any lettering is included, since the indirect method produces a reversed image.

SOURCE LIST

Crayola Craft Fabric Crayons, 1, 3, 7, 34

WHAT YOU NEED

Raised surface

Fabric, 60% synthetic or more

Crayons (Crayola Craft Fabric Crayons)

Masking tape

Iron and board

Scrap paper

THE PROCESS

1. Stretch and tape the fabric over the raised surface to be rubbed. You might want to brush off any dirt first.

2. Color the design with fabric crayons, stroking back and forth at one angle until the image is visible.

3. Remove the tape and lay the fabric, crayon side up, on an ironing surface.

4. Cover the colored area with clean scrap paper and heat set, step-pressing and using as hot an iron as the fabric will allow.

Basket Textures

This rubbing picks up the texture of woven basketry. Fabric was taped over an area of a basket, then rubbed with transfer crayon and heat set.

Fish

The fish is a crayon rubbing over a paper collage on tagboard. The collage was covered with muslin and taped to keep the layers from sliding. After rubbing, the muslin piece was backed with Wonder-Under. The fish was cut out and fused to a second piece of fabric.

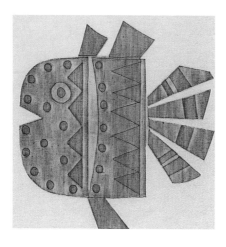

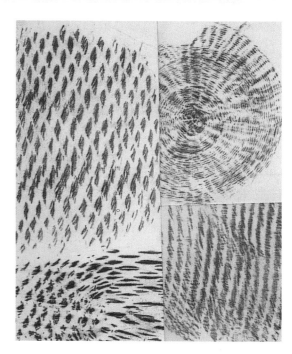

Gravestone Rubbings

Shown here are stone rubbings from a cemetery. Cloth was wrapped around grave markers and taped in place, then transfer crayons were used for the rubbings.

Indirect Rubbings

Indirect rubbings are made in the same way as direct rubbings, except that paper is substituted for cloth in the first step. The paper image is then transferred to cloth by heat setting. The result is a reverse image.

WHAT YOU NEED	THE PROCESS
Raised surface	1. Tape a sheet of smooth white paper over the surface of the area to be reproduced.
Smooth white paper	
Fabric, 60% synthetic or more	2. Color over the raised design with crayons, going back and forth until the image becomes visible.
Crayons (Crayola Craft Fabric Crayons)	
Masking tape	3. Remove paper and place it face down on fabric.
Iron and board	4. Transfer by heat setting for one minute.
Scrap paper	

Other Rubbings

Archaeologists sometimes record petroglyphic designs through the use of rubbings, since the reproduction offers an accurate record. Rubbings have been made from stone tablets, stelae, and incised stones for later study. The obvious advantage is that the original remains undamaged and in place. A wonderful tourist attraction at St. Martins-in-the-Field Cathedral in London provides a special room just for rubbings. All the materials you need are there, including the carved stones.

A cardboard panel can be prepared for rubbing by gluing different objects to it. White glue will secure ferns or leaves (vein side up), thick paper cut-out shapes, and string drawings. Or you could draw on heavy craft foil (not cooking foil) with a dry ballpoint marker or a paintbrush handle and use that incised line for a rubbing. Once you get started, you will find many possibilities within easy reach.

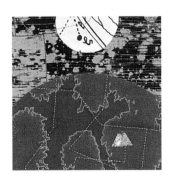

Linda S. Perry
Phases of the Moon, 30" x 42"
photo: Joe Ofria

A unique variation on rubbings is a technique Linda calls "rub printing." Starting with Masonite or a board, she uses a wide sponge brush to coat the board in white glue. She then places different things on the glue, such as rice grains, spaghetti, paper clips, puzzle pieces, or chicken wire. The board is left to dry for a day. Linda then pulls fabric over the dry board and tucks it under in a method she describes as "putting a bottom sheet on a mattress." Lumiere™ paint is spooned onto a foot-long piece of waxed paper and rolled out with a brayer. The paint-coated brayer is then rolled over the fabric, and the designs appear.

Linda S. Perry
Roka, 28" x 51"
photo: Joe Ofria

Linda's *Roka* incorporates prints of rice rubbings in gold and black. Other areas are rubbed over screens and meshes, combined with hand-painted fabrics, commercial prints, and metallic leaf.

DYE STICKS

Dye sticks bring out the mad artistic genius in us all. The brilliant colors in soft sticks readily adhere to cloth, inviting the budding Matisse into action. They are easy to use, non-toxic, and great for creating textures and strokes. Because they are portable, they are ideal for away-from-home work or projects for kids. The heat-set drawings are permanent on cotton, silk, or wool, but are not permanent on synthetics.

As dye sticks are fairly soft, it is difficult to get sharp or fine lines. By using them with stencils, you can achieve finer lines and sharp edges. Stencils are quick, easy to use, and readily controlled.

WHAT YOU NEED
Dye sticks
PFP fabrics (non-synthetic)
Freezer paper or other stencil
Scissors or craft knife
Iron and board
Pad of paper

THE PROCESS
1. Cut fabric and freezer paper to same size.
2. Draw a design on the dull side of freezer paper to make a stencil.
3. Using scissors or a craft knife, cut out the design and remove it. The background shape is the stencil; the open area will be colored.
4. Place the freezer-paper stencil, shiny side down, on fabric and press in place with a medium hot iron. Be sure cut edges have adhered well.
5. Details may be placed in the open fabric areas and ironed into place.
6. Color the open area with dye sticks.
7. Peel off the freezer paper, cover drawing with a sheet of plain paper, and heat set. (Use a medium hot iron for 30 seconds or more, moving the iron to avoid scorching.)

SOURCE LIST

Creative Paintsticks, 1, 3, 19

Delta Shiva Artists' Paintstiks®, 1, 34

Fabricfun Pastel Dye Sticks™, 1, 3, 34

Any sticky-backed or self-adhesive material can be used as a stencil. Try contact paper or stickers (the ones third-graders collect) as block-outs. Use freezer paper or masking tape to make lines and stripes. Once a color has been set, a new piece of tape can be added to cover a part of the first color, thus creating more complex plaids, checks, or lines. Crayons and dye sticks are versatile and can be used to add solid color, sketchy lines, textures, or polka dots to other fabrics. Keep them in mind when you need to rescue a print.

Lettering

Freezer paper letters, ironed to fabric, are colored over with dye sticks, crayons, or markers. The paper was then peeled away.

MARKERS

Markers do for fabric painting what spray cans do for graffiti: make it easy, colorful, and permanent. Anything is possible! There is a tremendous range available, so select permanent, non-toxic colors. If the fumes smell obnoxious, they probably are. Work only with good ventilation, and find a safe brand for the kids to work with. Markers are great for adding color to other projects, and you can also use them to draw and paint on cloth.

WHAT YOU NEED
Permanent markers
PFP fabric
Iron and board

THE PROCESS
1. Do freehand drawings or trace designs directly onto fabric.
2. Heat set each area as you work to avoid bleeding.

SOURCE LIST

Permanent Markers, 1, 4, 8, 16, 21, 34

Drawing with markers on loose fabric is difficult. To make the process easier, stretch the fabric taut, pin or staple it to a board, or stiffen it by ironing freezer paper to the back. As the fabric becomes saturated, colors may tend to bleed. To avoid this, dry and heat set the colors as you proceed. Test for washability, especially for large projects.

Elizabeth Jane Culbertson
T-shirt
photo: Betty Auchard

Eight-year-old Elizabeth Jane used a Sanford® fine marker for the clear and delightful drawing on her T-shirt. This marker makes the heaviest line of three Sanford markers, including extra-fine and ultra-fine.

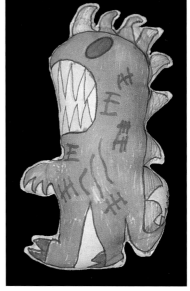

Daniel Hively
Toys
photo: Betty Auchard

Sharpie® pens, in the hands of six-year-old Daniel, were used to create the monsters. He colored his drawings with Niji Markers, after which they were heat set and sewn into toys by his grandmother.

TRANSFER PAPERS

using crayons, markers, oil pastels, and pencils

Crayons, markers, oil pastels, and pencils can be used directly on cloth, but many designers prefer a less risky approach. Drawings made on transfer sheets can be heat set to cloth. Marking pens and pencils transfer clearly, and crayons give brilliant color.

Any of these papers, designed for the inkjet printer, will work to transfer drawings to cloth in a simple, one-step process. Draw directly on the polymer surface, being careful not to scrape through the coating. Use either permanent or non-permanent markers or crayons. Trim away excess paper and transfer to cotton or cotton/poly fabric using a hot iron and as much pressure as you can muster. Peel while hot. The protective coating of the paper seals the drawing to cloth. Rinse in a dilute vinegar solution. As this is a one-step process, it produces a <u>reversal</u>. Finished pieces can be washed gently in cool to warm water.

PAROdraw

This is an iron-on transfer kit that lets you apply original art or drawings onto fabric. Lead or colored pencils, crayons, chalk, pastels, ballpoint pens, and non-water-soluble (permanent) marking pens can be used.

CAUTION: Do not use PAROdraw in a copier, which subjects it to heat.

PAROdraw is a two-step process in which your original is transferred to a specially coated paper. That paper is then transferred to cloth and the image will read correctly. Complete directions come with the paper. Finished fabrics can be washed, and are permanent as long as no bleach is used and the image is not ironed or dry cleaned.

SOURCE LIST

Affinity's High Definition, 20

Canon TR-101, 2, 6, 26

Jet-Ware!, 27

SOURCE LIST

PAROdraw™, 24

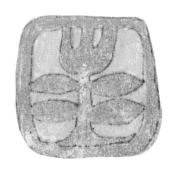

Pencil Drawing

A #2 pencil drawing on PAROdraw was heat set to cloth to make it permanent.

PAROdraw

Shown at left are two pieces drawn on PAROdraw, using crayons at the top and colored pencil at the bottom.

PAINTS

Artists who come to textiles from painting seem to develop a means of melding the two mediums. This more painterly approach is preferred by many fiber artists. <u>Acrylics</u>, while opaque, tend to stiffen fabrics somewhat, though they resolve the problem of printing or painting light colors on darks.

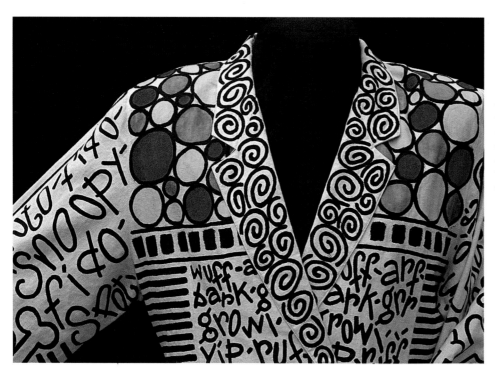

Heather Avery
Front of *Dog Jacket*
photo: Don Crodke

Heather's jacket utilizes direct printing with Deka® Textile Paints and stiff, short, flat brushes of different widths. On the front panel, the artist has included descriptions of dog sounds, and on the sleeves are dog names. The back states: "I've Got a Bone to Pick With You."

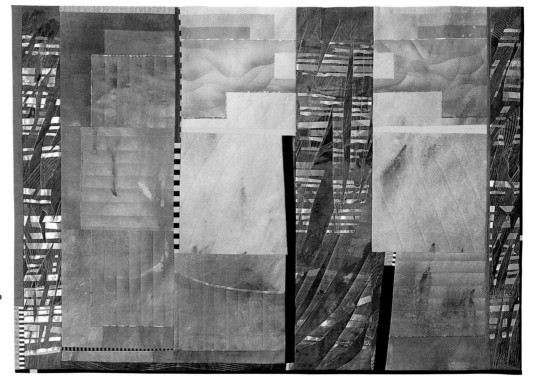

Elizabeth A. Busch,
Transformation, 43" x 62"
photo: Carina Woolrich

Many artists apply paint using an airbrush, often with stencils. In *Transformation* Elizabeth brushed and airbrushed acrylics directly to 7-oz. duck. She also used Prismacolor pencils with ribbon, textile ink, and metallic leaf on this machine-pieced, machine- and hand-quilted panel.

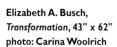

Mary Allen Chaisson
Women's Work, 62" x 45"
photo: Dennis Griggs

Mary has used textile inks,
acrylics, markers, and pigment to
create textures and colors on her
cotton fabric. Darker areas were
enriched with the slow-drying
Shiva oil sticks, and Tulip®
glitter paint was added last.

Nancy N. Erickson
Hand Shadows, 62" x 59¹/₂"
photo: Nancy N. Erickson

Working on whole cloth, Nancy
painted with fabric paints to
produce *Hand Shadows*. Her
method was to make a full-size
drawing on plastic, cut it out,
arrange the pieces until she was
satisfied with the configuration,
and then trace around the plastic
shapes onto her background fabric. She then appliquéd various
materials (satins, velvets, Mylar)
over parts of the surface to create
her textures and colors. Last, she
painted, and then incorporated
pearlescent powders with the
paints to enrich the surface.

CHAPTER 4

dye transfer

The wonders of dye transfer were vividly demonstrated to me as a teenager on a hot summer day. I sang in a small-town church choir, where we occupied leather-covered chairs at the minister's side. Directly in front of me sat Mrs. Beula K., a soprano of alarming proportions. After an endless sermon on a stifling hot and humid day, we rose to sing. As Mrs. K. arose, her dress, a flamboyantly-printed voile, peeled itself loose from the leather. There on the back of her dress was a perfect square of off-white fabric; transferred to the seat of her chair was a grand profusion of flowers! To this day, I am intrigued that heat and ample pressure will so readily transfer color, though I'm no longer convulsed with giggles that force me (from weakness, not piety) to my knees. All dye transfer is accomplished in a similar way. This chapter includes:

dye transfer with disperse dyes
disperse dyes with copiers
disperse dyes, other uses

DYE TRANSFER WITH DISPERSE DYES

Disperse dyes can be permanently transferred to any synthetic or part-synthetic fabric which can withstand heat setting. Cloth fibers open with heat, allowing the sublimation dyes to bond permanently. Dyes can be purchased already mixed (Deka IronOn) or in powdered form from Aljo manufacturing, Pro Chemical and Dye Company, or Spectrum Dyestuffs. They are water-based, washable, dry-cleanable, and do not change the hand of the fabric.

Dye transfers work best on white or light fabrics. Brilliance and permanence can be achieved with 100% synthetics, such as polyester, tri-acetate, and acrylic, though a 60% synthetic will work. Smooth fine fabrics (like satin acetate) will be more intense in color than coarse fabrics. Since direct ironing can melt some fabrics, a tissue-paper cover is recommended. Dyes transferred to natural fibers will not be as bright or permanent.

Along with the powders and liquids, disperse dyes are found in transfer crayons and in transfer ribbons for printers. Any heat transfer dye that is permanent and colorful on synthetics is probably disperse dye. Since commercially prepared disperse dye sheets are no longer available, we now have to paint our own. The sheets can then be transferred directly (right to the cloth) or indirectly (to other objects, natural forms, or to toner), and then to fabric.

Transfer sheets can be painted ahead of time, dried, and stored for use.

Deka IronOn transfer paint

Liquid Deka IronOn colors are ready for painting onto paper to make dye sheets. The six available colors can be intermixed, and transfers can be graphic or more painterly. Ready-mixed dyes are convenient, but the paints come in small quantities (one-ounce jars) and in sets of six colors only. I always end up with unused yellow (too light to show well on light cloth) and black.

WHAT YOU NEED

Deka IronOn Transfer Paint

Smooth white paper (copy or typing)

Bristle or sponge brush, 1" wide

Fabric on which to print (at least 65% synthetic)

Iron and board

Newsprint

Tissue paper

THE PROCESS

1. Apply Deka IronOn paint to smooth, white paper, with brush strokes going all in one direction. When dry, add a second coat by crossing the direction of the first coat. Thin coats will usually transfer only once; thicker coats several times.
2. Store dry papers in a box or folder away from light. Painted surfaces should not touch.
3. Cut out shapes from the transfer sheets.
4. Cover ironing board with newsprint and place fabric on board. Preheat iron to the highest setting the fabric will tolerate.
5. Place cut papers painted side down on fabric. Cover with a sheet of tissue paper or newsprint and iron carefully with a hot iron for 1 to 1½ minutes. You can also use a flat-bed dry mount press or heat press. Change tissue sheets as they become discolored.

SOURCE LIST

Deka IronOn Transfer Paint, 1, 3, 21, 22, 34

Shapes and images cut from sheets and heat-transferred to cloth give a graphic look with flat areas of color. For a more painterly, textured effect, colors can be mixed as you paint the sheets. Add brush strokes, swirls, or stippling, or scratch into the surface of the wet paint. All these variations will transfer to your cloth. As excess dye may fume or spread, additional layers of tissue will help absorb the excess.

**A sheet of paper covered with
design dye was scratched while it
was wet. A small rectangle of the
paper is shown transferred to a
hand-painted cloth.**

Disperse Dyes with Blocks and Stamps

Use a sponge or bristle brush to paint dye onto stamps or blocks. Or, paint the dye onto a
felt pad and press stamps directly onto it for transfer to cloth.

Shapes cut from dye sheets serve as stamps or printing plates. They can be heat transferred
to fabric singly or several at a time. First prints with disperse dye are often blurred, as excess
dye is transferred. Second or third prints will be the best, then they lighten as the dye is
depleted. Up to a half dozen prints can be made, depending on the thickness of the paint and
temperature of iron. Temperature may also affect the color.

Norma Wooddell
Medley

**Norma transferred a variety of
shapes and sizes from her painted
dye sheets. After heat setting,
she outlined each shape with a
permanent ink marker.**

Beach

**Dye papers snipped into small
shapes create transparent overlays and additional colors.**

powdered disperse dyes

Powdered <u>disperse</u> dyes are available in about twenty colors. They can be dissolved in water, then mixed with a thin gelatin base for painting on paper. The gum or gelatin adds a consistency (viscosity) which is more easily printed or painted onto paper. Dyes mixed from powders are essentially identical to liquid disperse dyes. The primary advantage of powdered dyes is the wide range of colors and the lower cost. The primary disadvantage is that caution must be used when handling powders.

WARNING: Health hazards from the powdered dyes are minimal, but avoid all eye contact and avoid breathing the fine dust. Wash yourself thoroughly after mixing or using the powders. Work with good ventilation, but avoid any breezes which could carry the powders. Wear rubber or neoprene gloves and safety goggles. Refrain from rubbing your eyes or face.

To mix a thickened dye paste the dye is first dissolved in hot water and added to the thickener. For a medium strength color, use:

 2 teaspoons powdered disperse dye

 $^{1}/_{2}$ cup hot water

Stir to dissolve thoroughly. Cool. Use as little as $^{1}/_{2}$ teaspoon dye for a pale mix, and up to 5 or 6 teaspoons for an intense or dark mix.

Thickeners are mixed according to the manufacturers directions, then the dye solution is added to the thickener. Aljo manufacturing suggests for 1 pint thickener:

 1 teaspoon gum thickener #3056 sprinkled over

 1 pint hot water

 Let stand, stirring often. Add $^{1}/_{2}$ cup dye solution to $^{1}/_{2}$ cup thickener.

ProChem recommends for 1 quart thin paste:

 $7^{1}/_{2}$ teaspoons PROthick F

 $1^{1}/_{2}$ teaspoons Metaphos

 or, for 1 quart thick paste:

 $7^{1}/_{2}$ tablespoons PROthick F

 2 tablespoons Metaphos

With both, dissolve in hot water. Mix and then cool. Add $^{1}/_{2}$ cup dye solution to $^{1}/_{2}$ cup thickener

Metaphos is the active ingredient in Calgon and other water softeners. Some recipes call for a drop of Synthrapol in the dye paste and a little vinegar or acetic acid in the thickener.

**SOURCE LIST
(FOR POWDERED
DISPERSE DYES)**

Aljo, 10

PROsperse, 31

**SOURCE LIST
(FOR THICKENERS)**

Aljo #3056, 10

Monagum, 31

PROthick F, 31

Sodium alginate, 3, 21, 33

Thickener, 41

**SOURCE LIST
(FOR OTHERS)**

Metaphos, 31

Synthrapol, 21, 33

Kris Vermeer
Original Drawing, 7" x 7"

Kris painted directly onto paper with liquid disperse dye, then transferred several prints to cloth by heat setting.

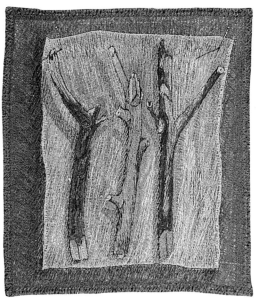

Richard Daehnert
Twig Relic III, far left, and
Twig Relic IV, left,
each 9¹⁄₂" x 8¹⁄₂"
photo: Sandra C. Walker

Using disperse dyes like watercolors Richard painted from direct observation onto a non-absorbent paper (vellum). When the paint was dry, he transferred the dye to polyester satin using a drymount press for one minute at 350° F. The fabric was then spray-mounted to the artist's canvas before being enriched and refined with an intricate tracery of machine stitching, used like colored drawn lines over the image.

commercially printed
disperse dye papers

The commercial printing of synthetic fabrics produces used dye papers, which have enough dye left in them for transfer. Available in the proximity of textile industries, these sheets are often sold as wrapping papers. I have found transferable wrapping papers from Korea and France, though I can identify them only by trying a transfer. The wrapping papers (and sometimes small gift bags) are usually thin and flimsy feeling. In Canada I found papers at florist shops—the big sheets (used to wrap large bouquets) are heavier and transfer beautifully to cloth. Heat set to synthetics, the transfers are permanent.

DISPERSE DYES WITH COPIERS

Dye sheets can be used with the black and white copier in a simple and wonderful process to create permanent detailed dye transfers. A dye sheet is placed face down on a copy and heat set which transfers color to the toner of the copy. The copy can then be used to make prints. Images will be reversed. Transfers from copies of photographs give a half-tone effect.

Barbara J. Mortenson,
Detail of *The Heart Conditions*
photo: Hank Jaffe

Barbara transferred images of hearts to polyester satin fabric in *The Heart Conditions*. After ironing disperse dye sheets to her photocopies, she heat set them to the fabric, then embellished the shapes with machine embroidery to create the very active lines surrounding the hearts.

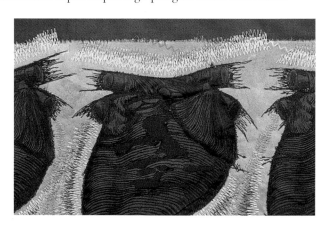

WHAT YOU NEED

Copy of original
Iron and board
Disperse dye paper
Fabric
Newsprint

THE PROCESS

1. Copy your drawing or photograph. The copy must have toner. (Some of the "improved" toners in laser copiers absorb less dye.)

2. Place copy face up on a smooth cardboard or a newsprint-covered ironing board.

3. Cut a piece of dye-coated paper the size of the copied image and place it color side down on the copy.

4. Press with a hot iron. Color transfers to toner, though it is difficult to see that it has adhered. Some color will also transfer to the background area of your copy and add a pale color over all. Peel the painted sheet off while hot.

5. Cut out the area you wish to transfer. The cut shape is important because the background may also partially transfer. For example, using a photo of a cat, cut a rectangle around it. When transferred, the linear part of the cat will be darkest in color, overlaid by a pale rectangle of the same color.

6. Place fabric right side up on an ironing surface protected with newsprint. Place copy face down on fabric and heat set. Image will be reversed.

Ritva

In these examples dye sheets were ironed over black and white copies to create permanent single-color transfers.

The first print may be blurry. Make up to a half dozen prints, depending on how thick a coat of dye was used, absorbency of toner, heat of the iron, etc.

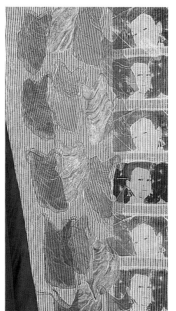

Barbara J. Mortenson
The Dance, 48" x 52"
Detail of *The Dance*
photo: Hank Jaffe

Dye transfer was used to add images to the pajama bottoms in Barbara's panel. For the words at the left of the panel, the artist first made a transparency of the script. The transparency was then flipped and copied. Disperse dye was ironed onto this reversed copy so the final image on fabric read correctly. The lettering offered a subtle and quiet message, and contrasted with the gaiety and color of the clothes, enhancing the concepts of concealing and revealing within relationships. The slips were colored with dye transfer, while faces are printed with the Print Gocco (Chapter 5) onto organza.

DISPERSE DYES, OTHER USES

Feathers

A dye sheet can be heat set to natural forms (feathers, leaves, ferns), which will absorb dye. The form can then be transferred as shown here.

Lettering

Draw letters on the white uncoated (back) side of dye sheets and cut them out for direct transfer; they will read correctly. Use stamp alphabets, which are already reversed, for any extensive wording. For most lettering, copy onto a <u>transparency</u>, and flip it to get a <u>mirror image</u>. Once transferred, it will read correctly. If your lettering is done on a computer printer, use a reversal option so you get a "backwards" print. Then make a photocopy of it, iron the dye sheet to the lettering, and print.

Natural Forms

Leaves, feathers, or other natural objects can be dye-transferred in two different ways. A leaf, used as the <u>block-out</u>, is placed on the fabric, and dry, dye-coated paper is placed color side down over the leaf for heat setting. The area protected by the leaf remains the original fabric color, surrounded by the dye color, making a <u>negative</u> print. Then the leaf (which will have absorbed some dye) can be used to make a <u>positive</u> print. Paper <u>cut-outs</u>, ferns, grass, or paper stars can be used as the silhouettes over which dye paper is used.

In a second method, apply dye directly to the back or veined side of a leaf. Let it dry. Place the leaf dye side down on fabric and cover it with tissue. Using the highest iron temperature the fabric will tolerate, iron over the tissue and the leaf to transfer the dye to cloth. Ferns, feathers, or leaves all offer interesting patterns, and even parsley and baby's breath can be ironed flat to make them printable. To have leaves available for winter use, some printmakers freeze a small plastic bag full. For variegated hues, apply several colors to a single leaf. When printing a series of images on one sheet, be sure to protect the printed area before making additional prints, unless you want to create overlays.

Leaves on Blocks

In the sample below left, leaves served as stencils with squares or rectangles of disperse dye sheets placed over the top to create negative shapes. A dye-coated leaf (violet) was placed on the background with orange paper over it; both colors transferred at once.

Leaf Prints

Leaves, inked with dye papers, transferred to synthetic cloth. At right, one leaf print has fumed.

Migrating Color

Disperse dye colors sometimes fume or migrate, as excess dye moves when released by heat. To take advantage of that tendency, try placing cut shapes (colored side up) on the fabric. Cover with tissue and heat set to spread the color past the area of resist. Use careful, circular ironing motions to help the colors spread to the sides. The stencil will protect the background color as dyes spread around it in a halo effect.

Screen Prints

Disperse dyes can be screen-printed onto paper to make transfer designs for cloth. The dye may require thickening to get the best consistency for printing.

Storing Unused Papers

Keep disperse dye sheets covered in a cool place. Separate sheets with tissue or scrap paper to avoid storing them face to face.

Second Transfers

The color intensity of subsequent transfers depends in part on the thickness of the paint and the amount of heat applied. Always try getting several prints. Dye colors on copies are most likely to provide a series of good transfers.

Other Dyes

Crayola Transfer Fabric Crayons can be used to make dye transfer papers. Color part of a sheet of typing or copy paper with solid areas of crayon. Cut out letters or shapes and heat transfer them to synthetic fabric (see Chapter 2, Crayon Transfer, page 50). Or draw, sketch, and scribble with crayons to create patterns and textures for transfer.

TROUBLESHOOTING FOR DISPERSE DYE PRINTS

Problem: Color does not transfer at all, or is pale.

Solution: Use higher iron temperature.

      Dye in sheets may be depleted by earlier use or age.

      If working from a photocopy, make sure your copy has toner.

      Use synthetic fabric.

Problem: Lines or spots appear in the color.

Solution: Apply pressure and heat evenly or use a heat press.

      Move the iron as you work.

      (The edge of sole plate or the steam vents may leave marks.)

      Paint papers smoothly, blending colors.

Problem: It is difficult to remove the dye sheet from the copy.

Solution: Reheat, then peel immediately. If it still adheres, use less heat next time.

Problem: The color migrates, giving a blurred image.

Solution: Experiment to determine the best heat, and time.

      Apply a thinner layer of paint, if hand painting.

      Use a heavier fabric which will absorb more dye.

      Use scrap fabric over the print to absorb excess dye.

      Avoid moving papers as you iron. Step press, lifting the iron.

Kathleen Deneris
Detail of *Well Preserved*
photo: Kathleen Deneris

The images of President Reagan, preserved under the Ball® Mason jar, were screen-printed on fabric by Kathleen using disperse dye. She started with the powdered dyes, dissolved in warm water and thickened with sodium alginate. She added more color to the panel with Crayola Transfer Fabric Crayons (also disperse) and heat set by ironing. The color suggested highlights or reflections on the glass. Individual heads were then appliquéd to the bunting pattern of the background.

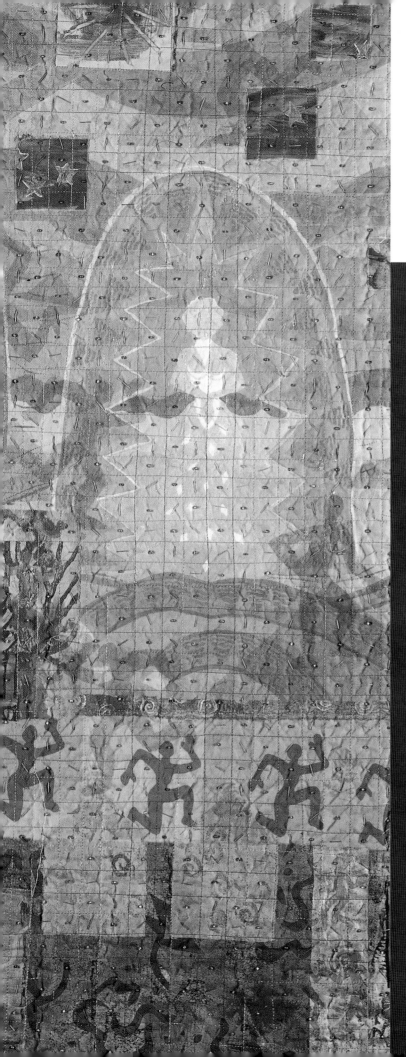

screen
printing

Multiples are compelling; it's hard to ignore anything repetitious. Our consciousness of multiples was sharpened by Andy Warhol's images of Marilyn Monroe and the Campbell's® soup cans. He increased our awareness of the repeated image, a concept already familiar to most quiltmakers. My own idea of multiples runs to the Dionne quintuplets, Tweedledum and Tweedledee, and 76 Trombones. None of the individual images is particularly intriguing; it is only when repeated that they pique our interest and take on new dimensions. This chapter includes:

general information for screen printing

quick screening

photographic screening

thermal imagers (copiers)

GENERAL INFORMATION FOR SCREEN PRINTING

Screen Printing Frame

Screen printing uses a rigid wood frame over which a polyester mesh is stretched taut and stapled or corded into place. The screen printing frame serves to spread paint in an even layer and to hold the stencil. While silk was once common, polyester filament is now preferred, since it will withstand the chlorine bleach used to remove the photo emulsion. When you have a choice, select a corded frame, as it makes tightening or replacing the mesh easier.

An 8" x 10" screen frame covered in 12xx to 14xx multifilament polyester mesh is a good starting size. A lower mesh size number means you will have a more open weave, less detail in the print, and greater ease in cleaning. A higher mesh size number (over 16xx) means a tighter weave, finer detail, and a tendency for paint to dry out more quickly in the screen. Anywhere within this range is good for fabric, on which very fine detail is lost anyway.

A new screen must be degreased, or thoroughly cleaned. Scrub with a powdered detergent, or use 2 tablespoons trisodium phosphate dissolved in 2 cups water. Rinse, then wipe with white vinegar and dry. Polyester is strong and can resist the scrubbing.

Unless you have an eager resident woodworker, it is usually less expensive in both time and money to buy a ready-made frame than to make one (however, the library has good references on silk-screen frame construction). The frame must be rigid and free of any give. Carefully treated, it will last for years. You are less likely to wear out a screen than you are to inadvertently poke a hole in it with an X-Acto® knife or scissors.

Squeegee

This flat, partially flexible tool is used to spread ink in a silk-screen frame. The traditional wood squeegee, which has an inset rubber or plastic flange, is less satisfactory for water-based paints, but some printers like its weight and rigidity. I prefer a simple one-piece plastic squeegee or spreader, about 6" long and tapered on the two long sides. It is easy to clean, inexpensive, will not warp, and can be cut into smaller pieces. To cut, score the squeegee on one side, then force it to break by bending it over a table edge. In a pinch, a credit card, a piece of illustration board, a scraper, or spreader will work but the plastic squeegee has just the right degree of flexibility. Various squeegees are available where silk-screen supplies are sold.

Screening Techniques

Place the PFP fabric on a smooth surface and set the screen on top. Spoon a small amount of paint into the screen on a protected or stencil area. Pull the squeegee over the screen, forcing paint through the open areas. Lift the frame. The cloth may stick to the paint on the screen, and you must peel it off carefully. Never rest your screen flat on the table, as paint may transfer. Lean it against the edge of a low, stable container (like a tuna can).

Printing requires practice. A squeegee held nearly parallel to the mesh gives a greater contact area and forces more paint through. Held more vertically, less paint goes through. Start with a 45° angle.

A squeegee narrower than the width of the frame may deposit excess paint in streaks or lines. To avoid this, the squeegee must work like a snow plow, always moving excess paint off to one side. Hold it at a slight angle to that side. After a print is made, all the paint should end up at one end of the screen and should not be left over open areas of the mesh.

Apples

The apples were printed from two freezer-paper stencils. Colors were finger-blended.

To avoid cleaning the screen when making color changes, move from light to darker colors (orange to red, green to blue) rather than the reverse. It is also possible to put two or three colors side by side in a screen to get a multicolored image. They stay clear for a few prints, but will gradually mix. Keep a roll of paper towels at hand. Clean up smears as they occur or they will find their way to your fabric.

Drying the Prints

Place wet prints on a large, flat piece of cardboard and carry them to a space where prints can be spread out to dry. Various clamps and devices for hanging prints take more time than they are worth. Most are designed for paper, which is rigid, and not for fabric, which hangs limply and folds. Laid out on a flat surface or floor, prints dry quickly and can then be lightly stacked. Prints must be heat set, but there is no hurry to do this. Add a second color after heat setting the first.

Clean-up: Removing the Paint

After printing, use the squeegee to remove excess paint from the frame. Any unmixed color can go right back in the jar. Wipe the inside of the frame with paper towels and remove all tape or stencils. Clean screens immediately after use, washing thoroughly in cool water (with a tooth brush). If you must leave it (for coffee or to answer a phone), put the frame under a running faucet. Paint may stain, but it shouldn't leave a residue. Hold the screen up to the light to make sure it is clean.

Fabric

Natural fibers, which will withstand the required heat setting, work best. Start with plain cotton or muslin. Eventually you'll want to try textures, like velveteen. Silks are difficult to handle, but backing them with <u>freezer paper</u> helps. White-on-white printed fabrics give a wonderful effect, since the background takes the color in a different way than the print. Stripes and polka dots add great pattern, and Ultrasuede® takes paint nicely.

Paints

A variety of paints is available, and most are water-based, heat-set <u>textile paints</u>. A yogurt-like consistency is needed for screen printing. Among the commonly used brands are Versatex, PROfab, Lumière, Deka®, Neopaque™, Speedball, and Createx™.

For the processes in this chapter you will need:
BASIC SCREEN-PRINTING SUPPLIES
Silk-screen frame
Squeegee
Water-based, heat-set textile paints
<u>PFP fabrics</u>
Tongue depressor or craft sticks (to dip paint)
Paper towels
<u>Iron and board</u> (or pad)
Pad of <u>newsprint</u> or scrap paper
Low, stable container (tuna can)

SOURCE LIST

PFP fabrics, 38

Squeegee, 1, 15, 22, 34, 35

Silk-screen frame, 1, 15, 22, 34, 35

Water-based, heat-set
textile paints, 1, 22, 23, 34, 36

QUICK SCREENING

Quick screen involves the use of quick, easy, and disposable <u>stencils</u>. My first awareness of stenciling was watching the wondrous transformation of a chocolate cake. A paper doily, placed on top of the cake, was lightly dusted with powdered sugar. When the doily was lifted, there appeared a frosty, delicate pattern in white. We are all familiar with prehistoric cave paintings in which hands served as stencils, over which colored pigments were daubed (or spat). Stenciling is luxuriously easy now, with <u>freezer paper</u> and Mylar.

freezer-paper screen printing

Screen printing with freezer-paper stencils takes just minutes. Freezer paper, ironed onto fabric, creates masked areas which are protected and unprinted. A silk-screen frame is placed over the stencil and paint is spread over the open area with a squeegee.

WHAT YOU NEED

Basic screen-printing supplies (page 70)

<u>Freezer paper</u>

Craft or X-Acto knife

Masking tape

THE PROCESS

1. Select a simple design (avoid fine lines) which will fit within the silk-screen frame.
2. Cut freezer paper the size of the silk-screen frame (one piece for each color to be printed).
3. Cut fabric the same size as the freezer paper. Set aside.
4. Tape the design to a flat, hard cutting surface. Tape freezer paper on top, plastic side down, and with an X-Acto, cut out all areas to be printed in a single color. Repeat for each additional color.
5. Center the stencil on the fabric, and adhere it to the fabric with a medium hot iron, using extra pressure at cut edges.
6. Place the fabric on a smooth cardboard or paper-covered work surface. Center the screen over the stencil.
7. Add paint and squeegee the color. Lift the screen.
8. Dry print, then remove freezer paper and <u>heat set</u>.

SOURCE LIST

Freezer Paper, 4, 5

X-Acto Knife, 1, 3, 22, 34

The printed area of the fabric should be covered with paint, but if the surface looks shiny, there is too much. Put the screen back down and squeegee with more pressure, forcing excess paint back into the screen.

After printing, lift the screen to check the print. If it is not clear, put the screen back down and reprint, adding more paint if necessary. Lift and check again. When the print is dry, peel off the freezer paper. Truthfully, I pull the freezer paper off immediately to see the results (although there is a risk of smearing the image). After heat setting the fabric, iron on a second freezer-paper stencil (for the next color). As the freezer paper is translucent, visual <u>registration</u> for the second color is not difficult.

Freezer-paper stencils are re-usable. After printing, wipe the excess paint off the paper before it is peeled from the fabric. Position it on the next fabric and set it with the iron. Stencils can be used six or more times, depending on the amount of heat applied.

Always do a test print. Air dry for two to seven days (read individual directions) before washing. Drying prints in direct sunlight before heat setting seems to increase their permanence.

Registration is essential for two-color prints or for a series that must be identical. Cut all fabrics and freezer papers to that same size, aligning corners. All stencils must be aligned on the

Fruit

Freezer-paper stencil. Finger blended deep colors at the edges.

original. Stencil corners are matched to fabric corners when the stencil is ironed on. That puts all the images in the same place on each block and will assist you in registering a second color.

The use of an <u>airbrush</u> with quick screen offers a different look—neither flat nor brushed, but soft and three-dimensional. Use several light sprays and dry them between coats to achieve strong color. Over-saturated fabrics tend to bleed or run under the stencil.

TROUBLESHOOTING FOR QUICK SCREENING

Problem: You can't see the original through the freezer paper.

Solution: Outline the original with black marker.

Use a light table or a window.

Problem: You can't remove the freezer paper from the fabric easily.

Solution: Iron was too hot; use lower temperature.

Problem: Paint oozes under the edges of the design.

Solution: Squeegee more gently, since paint is being pushed under the stencil.

Use toe of iron to press freezer paper firmly at cut edges.

Problem: Paint goes through fine fabric and smears.

Solution: Iron freezer paper to the back of fabric.

Place fabric on an absorbent surface (blotter or newsprint)

Hillary's Quilt, 36" x 34"

In this quilt two drawings by six-year-old Hillary Law were copied on the black and white copier, lines were darkened, and one figure was enlarged to keep the two close in size. Stabilized fabric was run through a copier, printing one figure at a time. They were dried and heat set. Colors were added using freezer-paper stencils cut the same size as the quilt blocks.

Frances R. MacEachren
Detail of *Incarus: Before the Fall*
photo: Alan M. MacEachren

Fran created this sun face using freezer-paper stencils. Blue line details on the yellow and orange rays were added the same way. All were printed using a silk-screen frame over the stencil with Speedball silk-screening paints.

CHAPTER 5

Dominie Nash
Makeover 2, 44" x 35"
photo: Dominie Nash

Dominie over-painted the dark
and light diagonals of her panel
using freezer-paper stencils,
air-brushing the color and shading
it. Straight lines, S-shapes, and
textures overlap to create
transparent patterns.

Linda MacDonald
Unknown Portrait Series 2
24" x 39"
photo: L. Melious

Linda airbrushed her intricate
designs using freezer-paper
stencils over hand-dyed fabrics.
With fabric tacked to an easel,
and working outside, she airbrushed black (at the edges) and
white paint. When these were
dry, she painted in detail and
color. For the background,
Linda used a passive-dye process
(with Procion **MX**™), which
involved putting fabric into a
bucket or dye bath and leaving
it until she added the soda ash,
which produced mottled and
textured fabrics.

Natasha Kempers-Cullen
Expectations, 48" x 48"
photo: Dennis Griggs

This is one of a series of panels by
Natasha called Saints and Sinners.
Natasha starts with a muslin panel
to which she collages her hand-
painted, screen-printed, sponged,
cyanotyped, and printed fabrics. A
final layer of tulle covers the panel.

Wendy Huhn
Joy of Ironing, 47" x 47"
photo: Carina Woolrich

Wendy's figures are printed from
freezer-paper stencils. Then black
and white drawings of aprons
were run through the photocopier,
heat set, hand colored, embellished
with puff paints, and adhered to
the patterned background fabric.
She then ran images of ironing
boards and irons through the
photocopier, added them to a
fusible backing, and adhered them
to the cloth. Rickrack, printing,
beading, quilting, stamping, and
stitching complete the panel.

Natasha Kempers-Cullen
Indiscretions, 48" x 48"
photo: Dennis Griggs

Natasha uses a variation of the plain paper silk-screen to make these reverse print figures. Starting with a freezer paper stencil, she squeegees over the paper side (plastic side down) so the paper sticks to the back of the mesh. She then screens with Inkodye™ resist. When it dries, she paints the background, then removes the resist. Additional stencils of rectangles are then used to overprint the area. The monoprint of sun and houses was made by spreading paint on Plexiglas®, drawing in it with a spatula, and pressing cloth onto the ink. At the bottom of the panel is a blue print for which lace and cut paper were used as block outs.

plain paper screen printing

This simple screen-printing method requires a sheet of typing paper or <u>newsprint</u> for the <u>stencil</u>. The stencil adheres to the screen, making it portable, so it is fast and easy to print multiples.

WHAT YOU NEED

Basic screen-printing supplies (page 70)

X-Acto or craft knife, or scissors

Paper (typing, copy, tissue, or newsprint)

Masking tape

THE PROCESS

1. Cut the fabric on which you intend to print. Place it over smooth cardboard or paper.

2. Cut a sheet of plain white paper the same size as your frame, to serve as your stencil.

3. Cut a simple shape, such as a bird, from the center of the paper. Toss the bird aside, keeping the background, which is now your stencil.

4. Place the stencil under the frame (against the mesh) and tape it at one end. Paper will cover all edges of the frame so no additional masking is needed.

5. Place the frame, mesh side down, on top of the scrap paper to make a test run.

6. Spoon textile paint into the screen.

7. Squeegee paint over open areas of the screen. See Screening Techniques on pages 69-70. Use two or three strokes for the first print. Paint will hold the paper stencil in place on the frame.

8. Lift the frame, resting one end on the edge of a tuna can.

9. If the image printed clearly, place the frame on your fabric and print. It will require more pressure or more strokes of the squeegee on fabric than on paper, as cloth absorbs more paint.

10. Repeat for additional prints, or clean up the screen immediately.

11. Dry prints and <u>heat set</u>.

Paper Stencil

The kind of paper used for the stencil will affect the character of the print. Hard-finish papers last longer than soft papers, but they can warp, and may allow paint to ooze under the edges. Tissue papers allow paint to soak through and add a textured pattern. As the tissue soaks up more paint, prints become progressively more textured. Rice paper, newsprint, copy paper, paper napkins, or construction paper will all work.

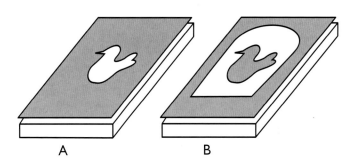

If you always start with paper cut the size of your frame you will cover all edges and allow for a "<u>well</u>" to hold paint. By cutting a bird from the center of that sheet as in A, you create a stencil for a <u>positive</u> print; that is, you will print the bird shape you have cut. If you use the bird as a stencil, you print the background, making a <u>negative</u> print. For that you need to mask the edges, as in B. Cut a second paper the size of the frame. From that paper, cut a shape which will define the edge of your print. The second paper will become a mat or a window around the bird. Allow at least 1" between the inside edge of the paper and the inside edge of the wood frame for a "well" to hold paint. Tape the mask to the underside of the frame, centering it. Make a practice print on paper to moisten the stencil and keep it in place; the screen is then ready to print on cloth.

Torn Paper

A soft or deckle edge can be created with a newsprint stencil. Cut paper the size of your frame, then (working in the center) either tear it by hand or draw on the paper with water, using a brush or your finger. As the paper soaks and softens, scrape away the wet paper with a fingernail. This paper stencil, taped to the back of your screen, will give a soft, complex edge and will last for 25 prints or more, depending on the paper used and the energy applied to the squeegee.

TROUBLESHOOTING FOR PLAIN PAPER SCREEN PRINTING

Problem: Paint spreads past the edge of the design.

Solution: Use a softer, more absorbent paper such as plain newsprint for the stencil.
              Squeegee with less force.

Problem: The image is pale, streaky, or only partially printed.

Solution: Use more paint.
              Take more strokes, or use more pressure.
              Hold the squeegee more parallel to the mesh.

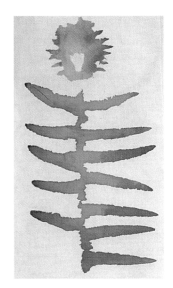

Sunflower

Torn paper stencils were accented with a second, darker color.

Jack Brockette
In the Moon When the Fish Were Many, 90" x 70"
Detail of *In the Moon When the Fish Were Many*
photo: Chuck Pawlik

Paper stencils need not be limited to small-scale work, as evidenced in this large panel. After laying out a 70" x 90" piece of white fabric on a huge table, Jack cut a stencil in the form of a spiral. Over the stencil he silk-screen printed the Mimbre fish designs, moving the 8" x 10" silk-screen frame from one spot to the next and sometimes letting one print overlap another. When the stencil was removed, the sharp-edged spiral emerged. Jack machine quilted in the white areas with white thread. With the righthand corner turned back (above), the quilting pattern shows clearly against the black backing fabric.

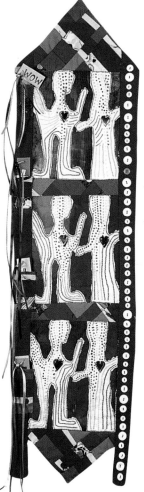

Karen Page
Apartment House, 30" x 12"
photo: Charles Neu

Karen's figures torn from newsprint provided the stencils for printing with Versatex. The individual prints were pieced with other fabrics, then embroidered and embellished. Ribbons, attached to a yellow plastic ring, can be pulled to reveal rubber-stamped messages and words.

Striped Bass, 17" x 26"

Printed from a torn newspaper stencil, the fish were printed using two colors of ink simultaneously on the screen.

A more durable and equally inexpensive block-out can be made from clear self-adhesive shelf or contact paper or a contact paper available at grocery or hardware stores (Con-Tact®, Magic Paper, etc.). One roll will make many block-outs. Use simple shapes and avoid detailed lines to start with.

SOURCE LIST

Contact paper, 5, 34

X-Acto knife, 1, 3, 22, 34

WHAT YOU NEED

Basic screen-printing supplies (page 70)

Self-adhesive clear contact paper

X-Acto or craft knife, or scissors

Masking tape

Old spoon

THE PROCESS

1. Cut a sheet of contact paper the same size as your frame.
2. Place the original design on a smooth surface and tape one edge in place. (Outline with a fine-point marker, if necessary, to make it more visible.)
3. Place contact paper (shiny or plastic side up) on top of the original. Tape.
4. Cut out the design using an X-Acto or craft knife. Peel, remove, and discard plastic layer from the areas to be printed.
5. Peel the stencil away from its paper base. Press the adhesive side to the mesh bottom (outside) of the frame, matching corners, and smoothing it into place.
6. Place the frame, mesh side down, on a smooth surface. Working inside the frame, burnish all cut edges with the bowl of a spoon until firmly adhered. The contact paper stencil now covers the bottom of the frame.
7. Screen your first print. Dry and heat set.

Cutting the Contact Paper

Work on a hard, smooth surface. Try to cut through just the clear plastic layer, leaving the paper backing intact. (On more intricate designs, the paper backing will help hold the design together.) Cut in a continuous line, pivoting at corners without lifting the craft knife from the plastic. If your cutting lines cross, paint may ooze through the cuts. Contact paper will stretch slightly if not pulled away from the paper with care. As you peel, attach one edge of the adhesive side to one edge of the frame (on the outside). Smooth it onto the mesh as you continue to peel.

Contact screens are durable and will most likely outlast your energy. To re-use them, wash away all excess paint and hang the stencil to dry. The stickiness seems to last, though eventually it will dry out. Store dry stencils by readhering them to the backing paper for re-use later.

When a run of prints is finished, clean the screen and check for any residue. Clean-up should be immediate and thorough.

Reversing the Image

This contact stencil method will give you a mirror image or reversal. To cut the contact paper and correct the reversal, follow the basic process with this exception: Put the contact paper, with paper side up, over the drawing and trace the original onto the paper. Turn the contact paper over, plastic side up, so the drawing can be seen through it. Cut and complete as before. The image will look reversed but, when applied to the mesh, it will read correctly.

TROUBLESHOOTING FOR CONTACT PAPER SCREEN PRINTING

Problem: Small folds or wrinkles at the cut edges of the film let paint leak through.

Solution: Contact paper was stretched as it was peeled or the X-Acto knife was dull.

          <u>Burnish</u> more firmly.

          Clean and dry screen, then clip (with scissors) into the wrinkle and overlap the cut edges

          like a dart. Don't clip your mesh!

          Squeegee away from, rather than into, the fold.

Problem: Fine lines appear past the edge of the design.

Solution: Avoid cutting past any corners or turns (lines allow paint to seep through).

          Cover lines with cellophane tape on the bottom of the frame (not on the inside).

Problem: Small spots or blurs appear in the prints.

Solution: Screen is not clean. Be sure to remove paint right after printing.

          Contact adhesive may be clogging the screen. Wipe mesh with solvent.

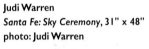

Jean Ray Laury
Details from the quilt *Listen to*
Your Mother

**Shown here are three blocks of a
quilt I'm making for my grand-
daughter who will be off to
college next year. Each block
contains a quote familiar to our
family, though these admonish-
ments seem universal.
I undoubtedly heard them and
passed them on. Contact paper
stencils were used to print the
backgrounds, silhouette the
mothers, and create the balloons.
Polka dots, squares, and triangles
were cut from contact paper and
stuck onto the screen before
printing. Freezer-paper stencils
were used for faces, hands, collars,
eyes, glasses, etc. Areas difficult
to align (such as the hair) were
hand-painted. Lettering was done
with large markers on paper, and
then Thermo-Faxed.**

Judi Warren
Santa Fe: Sky Ceremony, 31" x 48"
photo: Judi Warren

**Judi's panel utilizes an elegant
and subtle screen print done with
a contact paper stencil. After
printing the all-over pattern, she
painted landscapes of sky and
trees, which were then cut into
strips and reassembled with
gradually expanding strips of
blue. The parts were then
assembled and quilted.**

Other Self-Adhesive Papers

Stickers provide a great source of ready-cut designs. Remember that they will be <u>negative</u> prints. With a bear sticker, you will print the background (not the bear). Sticky-backed dots, ovals, labels, etc., all can be used as textures and patterns. Masking or cellophane tape can be similarly applied to either cloth or screen.

other stencils

Any material that will protect fabric from the application of paint can be used as a <u>stencil</u>, e.g., torn cardboard, thread, cut-outs from plastic bags. One common stencil material is Mylar.

Mylar

A thin sheet of Mylar will cut more easily than a thicker one. Most craft shops stock Mylar or similar stencil materials. A <u>spray adhesive</u>, such as 3M's Spray Mount®, on the back of the stencil keeps the stencil in place as you work, as does the two-sided tape. (Use the spray out of doors and avoid breathing any vapors.)

SOURCE LIST

Mylar, 3, 4

Stencil paper, 3, 4

CHAPTER 5

WHAT YOU NEED

Mylar (or other clear or translucent stencil material)

X-Acto knife

PFP fabric

Water-based <u>textile paint</u>

Stencil brushes

Pad of <u>newsprint</u>

Masking tape

Iron and board

THE PROCESS

1. Draw your design, enlarge or reduce it, and tape the final version to a hard surface.
2. Tape Mylar, shiny side up, over the design.
3. Cut out and remove shapes which are to be stenciled the same color.
4. Cut a new stencil for each additional color.
5. Tape the first Mylar stencil, shiny side up, on fabric. Tape both fabric and stencil in place.
6. Using a stencil brush, apply color to the open, unprotected areas.
7. Allow to dry and <u>heat set</u>.

There are dozens of variations and refinements to stencilling. Paint can be applied with <u>air-brush</u> or sponges, and almost anything can serve as a stencil. Elizabeth A. Busch's use of cards as stencils is one of my favorites. While Mylar and plastic are waterproof, cardboard works well. Masking or cellophane tape are great for creating plaids, stripes, or checks.

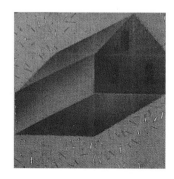

Elizabeth A. Busch
Persephone's Dream, 27¹/₂" x 34"
photo: Dennis Griggs

Elizabeth's use of stencils is not only highly effective, it is extremely simple. She placed index cards on the cloth to create protected and open areas, then added color with airbrush, moving the index cards as needed. Only the windows were cut specifically to a size and shape. The artist started her work by painting her canvas (7-oz. duck) with acrylic, and adding a grid with Prismacolor pencils.

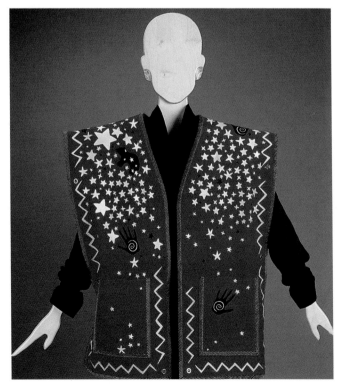

Mary Preston
Bear With Me
photo: Roger Schreiber

The star stencils in Mary's elegant vest were cut in a variety of sizes—sometimes one to a stencil, sometimes several. A white spiral was stenciled over the already dried black hand. To achieve opaque whites, Mary uses Lumière paints, formerly available through Cerulean Blue and now sold through Rupert, Gibbon and Spider under their Jacquard label.

Mary Preston
*For Entering the Forest
Where It Is Darkest*
photo: Roger Schreiber

Mary cuts thin Mylar (.003 inch),
shiny side up, for her stencils.
To hold them in contact with
the fabric and prevent slipping
she sprays the back with 3M
Spray Mount Artist's Adhesive
#6065, which leaves no residue on
cloth and lasts through several
clean-ups. She applies her paint
with a dauber, an inexpensive and
long-lasting tool made from two
4" squares of ¼" foam rubber,
one folded inside the other. The
outside piece is gathered up
around the folded piece and
secured with a rubber band. Her
enjoyment of myths and stories is
evidenced in this piece. Mary
combines stencils, stitching, and
piecing, along with three-
dimensional embellishments.
Lumière paints, used on the bear,
give a suede-like effect.

Mary Preston
Horse Power
photo: Roger Schreiber

After stenciling the dark stars
and moons on the sleeves, Mary
used the "wrong" end of her
paint brush to add a pattern of
dots around each one. The lines
of stitches were added with
embroidery floss.

Mary Preston
Phoebe, 26"
photo: Dane Gregory Meyer

Mary used stencils for the
moon and the stars of the snow
leopard's vest, the hawks on her
skirt and her paws. Features are
free-hand painted.

Pro-film and Ulano

Pro-film and Ulano consist of a layer of film adhered to a paper backing. Both must be meticulously cut with an X-Acto or frisket knife. Then the stencil portion of the film is melted into the mesh of the screen using a solvent. For Pro-film use acetone, for Ulano use Ulano adhering solution. This is a touchy process but gets easier with practice. These films produce long-lasting screens which can be removed with solvents. I learned to screen print using this process, and printed with oil-based paints, which were cleaned with mineral spirits. It is wonderful to now have non-toxic, water-based paints and new application methods which eliminate most uses of solvents.

SOURCE LIST

Pro-film®, 1

Ulano®, 1, 22, 34

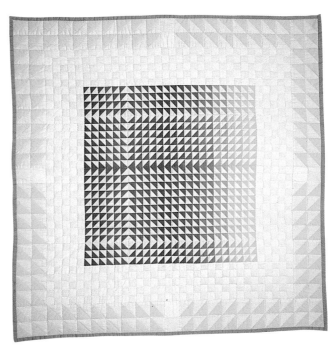

Jean Ray Laury
Half Way Around, 40" x 40"

The dominant colors in this quilt—yellow and violet, move half way around the color wheel, and mix in gradations to reveal the resulting golds, browns, and greens. The stencil was cut from Pro-film, a product I no longer use. But these long-lasting screens are still sharp edged and work perfectly with water-based paints. The small triangles were printed in panels about 6" x 8", and were then cut into smaller pieces as needed. Each change in color or direction indicates a different print. The wide border is white screened on muslin.

Hallie O'Kelley
Noah's Ark, 40" x 40"
photo: Charles O'Kelley

The images in this quilt were screen printed using two kinds of stencils. For the more complex stencils Hallie uses Ulano Sta-Sharp® knife-cut film. For simpler shapes she uses a 3 mil. plastic (from a hardware store), which is easily cut and will lie flat. With her fabric panel pinned to a working surface to keep it from shifting, she printed the sky, flood, Noah, and the other figures. Hallie uses Colortex extender or base, to which she adds her pigments.

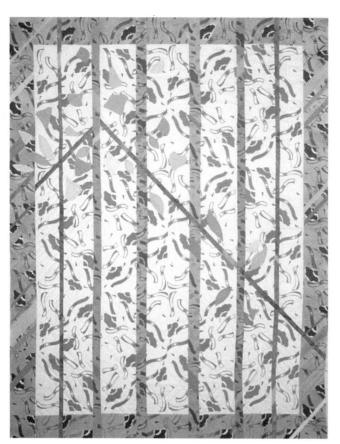

Judi Warren
Summerharp, 64" x 54"
photo: Judi Warren

Judi printed the silk-screened yardage for *Summerharp* using Ulano film melted into silk-screen mesh with acetone. Some of the white fabric was printed with blue and violet, some with red and violet. Judi then painted the background of the red/violet yardage with a peach color, reserving that for the border and vertical strips. The fabrics were pieced into vertical rows, with diagonal intersections. A pearlescent white (Createx) was added to the border and painted over everything, so the images show through the iridescence. The final step, before quilting and finishing, was the addition of the green shapes.

Tusche and Glue

The tusche and glue method has special appeal for anyone who enjoys a direct, painterly approach. Tusche (actually a lithographic ink) is an oil-based liquid painted directly onto the mesh. When dry, the mesh is coated with a thinned water-based glue, which is resisted by the tusche. When the glue is dry, the tusche is removed with a <u>solvent</u>, leaving the glue in place and the painted areas open. Printing with oil-based ink creates a <u>positive</u> print of the original tusche painting. The liquids used have changed over the years, but the term "tusche and glue" has stuck.

For the water-based paints we now use on fabric, this process is reversed. A water-soluble substance is used first, then the oil-based substance. Companies which market screen-printing supplies also sell the tusche and glue (or Hunt Speedball Drawing Fluid and Screen Filler).

SOURCE LIST

Glue (screen filler), 1, 22, 34

Tusche (drawing fluid), 1, 22, 34

WHAT YOU NEED

Tusche and glue (or drawing fluid and screen filler)

Brushes

Silk-screen frame

Masking tape or <u>contact paper</u>

THE PROCESS

1. Paint a design with a water-based drawing fluid on either side of the mesh, and let it dry.
2. Paint screen filler on one side of the mesh to cover the design and let it dry.
3. Wash out the drawing fluid, using a toothbrush if necessary on stubborn spots. Dry.
4. Mask the edges and print using water-based textile paints.
5. Clean out the paint.
6. Remove the filler (as specified).

Place the frame flat, to keep the drawing fluid from running. If you paint on the inside of the frame, your image will not reverse, but you will need to prop the frame up off the work surface. If you paint on the outside, you will print a <u>reversal</u>. Use a small- to medium-size brush, depending on the amount of detail you want. Brush strokes and fluid lines will be reproduced.

Follow the directions for the particular filler you purchase. It may be removed at a different temperature than the drawing, or it may require another <u>solvent</u>. For example, Hunt Speedball Drawing Fluid is removed with cool water, while the screen filler is removed with hot water and detergent. Remove all traces of both materials from the screen when you finish printing.

TROUBLESHOOTING FOR OTHER STENCILS

Mylar
Problem: Paints have smeared.
Solution: Use less paint.
             Use an adhesive-backed stencil to prevent sliding.
             Brush gently, so the stencil is not jarred.
             Stencil may have picked up paint on the back.
Problem: The edges appear uneven or ragged, lacking sharpness.
Solution: Re-cut the stencil. Edges must be cut cleanly.
             Remove any paint build-up on the edge of the stencil.

Pro-film
Problem: Image is lost or incomplete.
Solution: Film was not completely adhered.
Problem: Edges are soft, fuzzy, nondescript.
Solution: Too much solvent used in adhering.

Tusche and glue
Problem: Image is barely visible.
Solution: Drawing fluid was not completely washed out.
Problem: Background is not clear or free of color.
Solution: Too little filler was used.

PHOTOGRAPHIC SCREENING

Of all silk-screen methods, the most magical is photographic screening. It is a direct-contact method, meaning that some opaque substance must come between sensitized screen and the energy source during exposure.

Photographic screens expand the print-making potential for text, fine details, and photos. Well suited to multiples, this process has many commercial uses. Prepared screens are long lasting and can be stored for later use. This section includes light- or heat-sensitized screens on which images can be exposed.

In this process the screen itself is painted with light-sensitive chemicals. It is dried in a darkroom, then exposed to sunlight or artificial light. Any area left open to exposure will develop and become the <u>block-out</u>. Those areas which remain unexposed will wash out, and paint will later be squeegeed through them. Exposures are made with a <u>direct-contact frame</u>. Anything opaque enough to inhibit sunlight can be used to create the stencil.

With photo screening, everything from snapshots, drawings, invitations, old love letters (or new), family photographs, and silhouetted <u>cut-outs</u> can be used. Try weeds, leaves, announcements, or maps. The simple processes given here require no special photographic equipment or darkroom facilities. Dozens of books have been written about photo-screen printing, directed primarily toward oil-based inks on paper. The methods described here are for water-based <u>textile paints</u> on fabric.

Imagine that your screen is coated with light-sensitive emulsion. If you spread your hand out over the dry screen in sunlight, the hand would inhibit the passage of light. After a few seconds you would rinse the screen with a garden hose or faucet to stop the developing. The area of emulsion covered by the hand would wash away, but the background would be firmly set on the screen. You would print an image of your hand. Photo screening is a <u>positive</u> method. What you see (on the screen) is what you get (in the print).

Photo emulsion with dichromate sensitizer is favored by many fabric artists because it facilitates the use of photographs and multiples. The process is relatively easy and inexpensive. Most of the information given here refers to the dichromate emulsion, but a diazo emulsion is also available. It contains different chemicals but works similarly: it has a longer shelf life after mixing, it can be left on the screen for a longer time before exposure, and it requires a special remover (Naz-Dar Encosol 3 or Speedball Photo Emulsion Remover). I like working with Hunt Speedball Photo Emulsion because it is relatively simple and requires only household bleach to clean it.

Photo emulsion screening is done in one of two ways: photo emulsion screen printing or direct emulsion with photo enlargement. Read all directions before beginning.

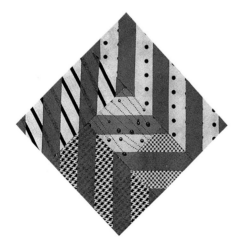

WHAT YOU NEED

Basic screen-printing supplies (page 70)

Photo emulsion

<u>Positive</u> image

Black fabric

<u>Glass</u> or Plexiglas

Flexible foam pad

Rigid surface

<u>Contact paper</u> or wide masking tape

Panel or board on which to print

Household chlorine bleach

THE PROCESS

1. Prepare the original.
2. Measure and mix the emulsion.
3. Spread the emulsion onto the screen and dry in darkness.
4. Prepare a <u>direct-contact frame</u>.
5. Place the dry emulsion screen on top of the black fabric (mesh touching fabric), with the stencil (block-out, or transparency) on top of the screen.
6. Put glass over the image to keep lightweight objects from moving in the breeze, and to keep transparencies from curling in the sun.
7. To develop the emulsion expose for 6 to 20 seconds in sunlight, or 10 to 20 minutes with floodlamp.
8. Immediately wet both sides of the screen with water to stop development.
9. Continue running water over the emulsion until the image area (unexposed emulsion) has washed clear.
10. Wipe and dry the wood frame and lay it flat to dry in the shade.
11. When it is dry, mask the open edges on the outside of the frame using masking tape or contact paper.
12. Place PFP fabric on a flat surface covered with paper or smooth cardboard.
13. Print using Screening Techniques (pages 69-70) and water-based textile paints.

SOURCE LIST

Advance DM-888 Photo Emulsion®, 1

Holden's Diazo™, 1

Hunt Speedball Photo Emulsion, 1, 22, 34

Naz-dar, 1, 22

Speedball Diazo, 1, 22

Preparing the Positive Image

Photo-screen printing requires a <u>positive</u> image, not a <u>negative</u>. Start by using a few leaves or a fern as the <u>block-out</u>. After following all steps, your leaves will be printed in color. Most leaves and flowers will be opaque enough to produce an image. Very fine stems, or the beard on wheat, will not produce a sufficiently strong block-out.

Paper cut-outs work well. Cut any shape from construction (or similarly opaque) paper and use it in the contact frame. Or use any handy opaque object: scissors, spatula, comb, etc. Remember, the form that inhibits sunlight is the form that will be printed.

To work with photographs or words, you will need another step. The image must be put onto a clear background—an acetate or <u>transparency</u>. Select a photograph which has strong contrast, deep shadows with areas of white, and make a photocopy. Cut away backgrounds, remove any unwanted guests, duplicate one person, enlarge or reduce the image. Shrink your big brother (bringing him down to size) or enlarge your mother-in-law. (That's not the same as blowing her up!) The altered image is then copied onto a transparency (using the black and white copier or printer). This gives you a positive (the opposite of a photographic negative). What appears in black on the transparency is what will print in color.

Check your copy before making a transparency. If the original is pale, the transparency may not be dark enough to block sunlight. Two transparencies, placed one over the other and taped together at one edge, will make it more light-resistant. Since copies vary slightly in size from the originals, make both transparencies from the original.

Anything you can photocopy can be put onto a transparency: drawings, hand-written or stamped words, school pictures, diplomas, traffic citations (not your own, of course), and hand prints. For a stronger black and white photo image, have a <u>Kodalith</u>® made. If it is made on a transparency, you expose directly from it. Otherwise, make a transparency of it. This will mean an extra errand and extra cost, so first try working with your photographs as they are.

Photo-sensitizing emulsion requires careful handling, as it contains ammonium dichromate. It comes pre-mixed in liquid form with the dichromate diluted 1 part to 8. You dilute it further in a mixture of 1 part dichromate to 4 parts emulsion. About a teaspoonful of the mixed emulsion will cover a small screen, so you only need a minute quantity. Working with liquids avoids any breathing of powders, the greatest hazard posed by this chemical.

Read all precautions or warnings which come with the packaged emulsion. The substance is mildly toxic, so avoid skin contact or ingestion, and no kids in the work area. Goggles are recommended. Store the sensitizing liquid away from heat.

Photo-sensitive emulsion comes in two parts: a yellow, watery light-sensitive liquid and a blue, viscous liquid which acts as a thickener and spreader. (Some brands may come with a third solution to add color to the mix.) I like Hunt Speedball Emulsion, because the yellow and blue, when well mixed, turn a dull green. Since it is difficult to measure the thick emulsion, pre-measure and calibrate a container with water. For a 5-tablespoon batch, put 4 tablespoons of water in a small jar. With a marker, indicate the height of the water line. Measure 1 more tablespoon and again mark the line. Empty and dry the jar. Pour emulsion directly into the jar to the first line, add sensitizer to the second, and mix. (Specific proportions and directions accompany each emulsion.)

Once the two parts are mixed, they are light-sensitive. Keep the mixed emulsion in a closed jar, covered with foil or black plastic. It can be stored for a week or two, depending upon temperature. It will last longer (up to a month) in a refrigerator, but don't store it there if you have kids in the house. Mix only the amount needed, or use the excess within a few days. Just 5 tablespoons of emulsion is enough to coat a half-dozen screen frames. To dispose of leftover emulsion, dilute it in several gallons of water, then flush it down the drain while running lots of water with it. If you have a large amount of mixed emulsion, which is unlikely, let it dry out in the jar. Then cap it, label it, and dispose of it at your local toxic waste site.

Applying the Emulsion

While emulsion is light-sensitive, you have several minutes to spread the emulsion on the screen. Use subdued lighting, and work at a normal pace, but don't leave the whole thing while you answer the phone.

Pour 1 or 2 teaspoons of emulsion on the outside of the screen. Using a credit card or a small squeegee, spread the emulsion evenly over the mesh. Scrape in both directions and return any excess to the jar. Turn the frame over, squeegee, and scrape off any excess. Briefly hold the frame up to the light. Dark areas indicate uneven or thick emulsion. Scrape off excess. If you see pinholes, add more emulsion. The goal is to spread a smooth, thin, even coat over the mesh.

Drying the Emulsion

Dry the screen in a <u>darkroom</u>, laying it flat. A small fan speeds up the drying time, so obviously a closet is better than a box if time is important. Optimum drying temperature is 76°. Use a hair dryer on air only. It takes from twenty minutes to over an hour to dry the emulsion, depending on its thickness, the temperature, humidity, and air movement.

Some emulsion directions recommend the application of a second coat after the first is dry. I never use more than one coat. For big-time production, a second coat may make the screen more stable.

Exposing the Image

When the emulsion is dry, place the screen, open side up, with mesh touching the black fabric. The image, or <u>positive</u>, goes directly onto the mesh with a piece of <u>glass</u> or Plexiglas on top. While exposure can be made on either the inside or the outside of the frame, I suggest using the inside, since that lets you view the image as it will print with no reversal. It also places the emulsion surface against the black fabric, ensuring that no light can get beneath it. See illustration below.

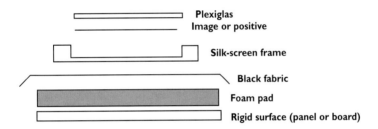

Plexiglas
Image or positive
Silk-screen frame
Black fabric
Foam pad
Rigid surface (panel or board)

If your positive is larger than your screen (for example, a branch of leaves) and the design is going to run off the edge, you will have to expose it on the outside of the frame. Fill the screen cavity with a piece of foam pad cut to fit, flip the frame, and place the <u>block-out</u> directly on top of the emulsion-coated screen. Glass goes on top of that. The image or block-out must make contact with the emulsion. For sun exposure, use a thumb on each side of the glass if necessary to hold it secure, remembering that your thumb will also block light.

For best results, expose the image as soon as the emulsion is dry. (With diazo emulsion, the coated screen can be left much longer before exposure.) Emulsion will look shiny when wet, dull when dry. If a sudden change of weather or the arrival of guests forces you to postpone exposure, store the dry frame in a black plastic bag in the darkroom overnight. Optimum time for use with dichromate emulsion, however, is within six hours. Exposure is the crucial part of a successful screen print. It is safer to under-expose a screen than to over-expose. The first can be easily removed and re-done; the latter cannot. Once the emulsion is dry, exposure can be accomplished in either of two ways: by sunlight or bulb exposure.

Exposure by Sunlight

I prefer the immediacy of sunlight; the results are known within a minute or two. Practice helps, but there is ample leeway to get good results while learning. Variables include the time of year, time of day, clarity of the air, and thickness of the emulsion. On a bright, clear summer day, at high noon, I expose for five to eight seconds, the least time I've ever needed. The most

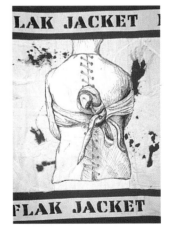

Kathy Weaver
Detail of *Flak Jacket*
photo: Nelson Armour

Kathy's jacket utilizes silk-screen printing for the words and messages. Her drawings are combined with piecing, appliqué, and quilting.

time (under an overhanging roof during a downpour) was 60 seconds. So most sunlight exposures can be done within that range. On dark wintry days you may have to switch to bulb exposure. There will be an occasional failure, but you'll soon learn to estimate exposure time.

Exposure by Bulb

You can use an ordinary clear household bulb (150 watts) or a #1 photo floodlamp (250 watts) in place of sunlight. An aluminum pie plate or tray may be used to create a reflector, to help direct the light onto your screen. Expose as follows:

Light source	floodlamp	household bulb
For small screens, 10" to 12" long:		
12" from screen	10 minutes	45 minutes
For larger screens, 20" long:		
17" from screen	20 minutes	1 hour, 30 minutes

Move the light source farther away from large screens so light hits all areas of the screen evenly. My preference for sunlight is based on my experience that bulb-set emulsions seem harder to remove. Still, some screen printers prefer using bulbs, and consider the use of sunlight too iffy.

Washing

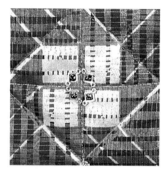

Immediately after exposure, spray the screen with water on both sides to stop further developing. You may see a milky version of your image where it has been exposed. It is important to wash out all the unexposed emulsion, as only the cleared areas will print. Spray on the inside of the screen if your exposure was made on the inside. Tepid water is recommended, but cold water works too. I do this part outdoors with a spray-nozzle hose, as pressure sometimes helps to remove unexposed emulsion. Water does get splashed around, so if you must use a bathroom, rely on the tub rather than the sink. The emulsion should disappear in all unexposed areas within a few minutes. If the design does not clear, continue spraying or try warmer water. Don't confuse clearing with the pale image that shows but is not yet washed out. With a stubborn screen, I've sometimes used a hard spray from a garden hose for 5 to 10 minutes, and eventually it loosened. Hold the screen up to the light to make sure areas have cleared completely.

When the image is clear let the frame dry out away from the sunlight. Wipe the wood frame with a towel. The emulsion may be slightly gelatinous, so be careful not to touch it. On a warm, breezy day, drying will take 10 to 15 minutes.

Printing

There will be spaces at the edges of the exposed screen that need to be masked with tape or contact paper. Place masking tape on the outside of the frame. This protects the fabric and creates a <u>well</u> to hold paint. Follow the techniques for printing on pages 69-70.

Test a print on paper, register the design, if necessary, and print, following directions at the beginning of this chapter. The photo screen can be used for dozens and dozens of prints. If your back begins to tire, wash out the screen, let it dry, and resume printing later.

Removing the Emulsion

If you wish to retain the design, the photo emulsion will last indefinitely. Your quilt label with name and photo may be something you wish to keep. To save it means the screen cannot be used for anything else.

Exposed emulsion can be removed from the mesh so a new design can be applied. Remove all paint and wash the screen before you start dissolving the emulsion. Removing the emulsion is easier if done within a few hours. As time passes, the emulsion gets more difficult to remove. If left too long, the image is permanent. "Too long" depends on initial exposure, thickness, and humidity. Emulsion is removed with household chlorine bleach or with special remover.

Fill a flat plastic tray such as a photographic tray or cafeteria tray with a thin layer of water ($1/2$" is adequate). Place the frame, mesh side down, in the tray. When the inside is wet, pour household chlorine bleach directly into the frame opening. Most directions call for 2 parts water to 1 part bleach, but I know of no one who actually measures. Soak the frame for 3 to 5 minutes, then scrub with a brush. Rinse in warm to hot water. The emulsion should wash out. If it does not, re-immerse it in bleach for a few minutes and, if necessary, scrub more vigorously. If it is stubborn, continue to soak and scrub, using a little trisodium phosphate on stubborn spots. If your frame is covered in silk (not polyester), this process will melt the silk.

The undeveloped emulsion, which has washed out and is now diluted in the bleach and water, should be diluted further and flushed into the drain with lots of water. Every agency I checked with regarded this amount of chemical as negligible. However, it is important to read all precautions and observe your local and state regulations regarding disposal.

Photo emulsion screens are often difficult to clean out—the emulsion may "set" and refuse to budge. When I talked with a chemist at Speedball, he recommended the following:

1. Soak the screen in the chlorine solution for only five minutes (too much time will actually set it).

2. Use screen remover.

I tried both Speedball Emulsion Remover and Naz-Dar Screen Wash, though neither helped on stubborn screens. I have cleaned scores of screens successfully—and there was a time when I wouldn't have considered abandoning a screen because it was too hard to clean!

I like Sharon Heidingsfelder's approach. She assumes all photo emulsion screens are permanent, and makes no effort to clean them for re-use. The mesh, however, can be replaced on any screen.

Screen printing allows the special pleasure of making gifts that are both personal and funny. I look for pre-finished articles, like hand towels, dish towels, sweatshirts or T-shirts, handkerchiefs or socks. Pot holders make easy projects (and always fit).

TROUBLESHOOTING FOR PHOTO EMULSION SCREEN PRINTING

Problem: The image washed out entirely after exposure.

Solution: Screen was underexposed: increase the exposure time.

Problem: It is difficult to remove the emulsion from the screen after exposure.

Solution: Hose or wash with greater pressure for a longer time.

Use warmer water.

Screen may be overexposed. Remove emulsion and try again.

Problem: Emulsion cannot be removed from mesh with bleach after printing.

Solution: Use fresh household chlorine bleach, full strength.

Replace the mesh.

Problem: The print is spotty or unclear.

Solution: Screen may not be clean. Clean it again. Degrease.

Dust may have settled on the wet emulsion, creating spots.

Paint or emulsion from an earlier print may be blocking the mesh. Force it open using pressure on the squeegee.

Use more paint, flooding the image before squeegeeing.

Problem: The image is smeared.

Solution: Avoid sliding or moving the frame while screening.

Check the back of the frame for paint smears.

Make sure the mesh is taut.

Ellen Oppenheimer
Labyrinth #8, 76" x 76"
photo: Jan C. Watten

In Ellen's remarkable work, photo emulsion screen printing is used for the four large designs. She first printed stripes on muslin, then over-dyed them. Blue-violet stripes were dyed in red. Next, she pieced the design from her striped fabric, also piecing the Greek key and zigzag borders, which were printed in purple and over-dyed.

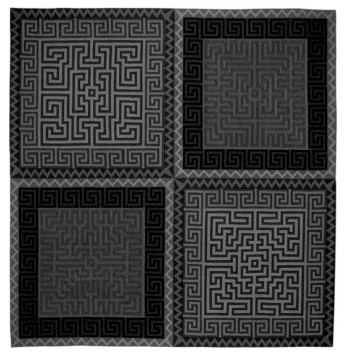

Barbara Sweeney
Detail of *Shells*

Using a photo emulsion screen, Barbara printed the linear shell patterns onto her fabric. She then hand painted the material with Procion H® fiber reactive dyes to add color to the background.

Ellen Oppenheimer
Detail of *Log Cabin Maze*
photo: Jan C. Watten

Using commercial fabrics of black and white stripes, Ellen photo silk-screened over them, "top-dyed" the fabrics, and pieced them into the active patterns of her composition.

Patricia Autenrieth
Chameleon, 43" x 42"
photo: Patricia Autenrieth

Patricia screen printed her own portrait using multicolored and patterned backgrounds. The portraits are printed in many colors, including white, with silhouettes of the head overlapping other screen-printed heads. Zigzag stitching around some silhouettes makes the overlays show up more clearly.

Sharon Heidingsfelder
Allegheny Moon, 78" x 78"
photo: Sharon Heidingsfelder

Sharon used photo silk-screen prints in several colors for many of the specific pieces needed for this design. She has developed a double-stencil method for printing just the sizes she needs. Her stripes, for example, might fill her silk-screen frame, but if she needs a triangular shape, she cuts a freezer-paper stencil to that size. The paper stencil gets taped under the screen so that a triangle of stripes is produced. This not only avoids wasted fabric but also provides a template-like shape and seamline for piecing.

Elizabeth A. Busch
Alert!, 52" x 37½"
photo: Dennis Griggs

A life-size doe, photo silk-
screened onto acrylic painted
canvas, watches warily in *Alert!*
Above the panel of the deer are
two hand-painted scenes. Each is
a watercolor-like painting on
muslin. This panel is the tenth in a
series of which *Hunting Game* is
the first.

Elizabeth A. Busch
Hunting Game, 62½" x 45½"
photo: Dennis Griggs

This whole-cloth panel was
painted with acrylics, then divided
into a grid pattern using Prismacolor pencil lines. Only the red/
white pattern of squares is a pre-
printed fabric. In Elizabeth's work,
the alert does in the border are
photo emulsion silk-screen,
printed in mirror image. House
shapes are airbrushed, as are
parts of the border. This piece
was the first in a series which
was a response to a Maine
hunting accident.

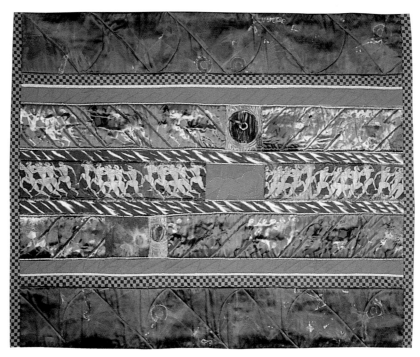

Jo Ann Giordano
Men Who Run, 37" x 47"
photo: Jo Ann Giordano

Using a print of Greek marathon runners, Jo Ann made both positive and negative images from that print. Her panel is less a comment on jogging than it is on men's fear of commitment. Using photo silk-screen, she printed the positive figures in some areas (with textile paint) to contrast with the negative prints (where she discharged the background) in others. A detail of the quilt is shown on page 157.

Elaine Anne Spence
Front of *Jimmy and Me*
Back of *Jimmy and Me*
photo: David Browne

When Elaine found a commercially printed fabric of her hero, James Dean, she was inspired to get the two of them together. Her jacket combines a print of Jimmy with a screen print of herself appliquéd next to him. A film strip is made up from a series of heat transfer images of the "stars." A cut-through technique is used to let the photos show through open areas of the dark blue Ultrasuede.

M. Joan Lintault
When the Bee Stings, 95" x 87"
Detail of *When the Bee Stings*
photo: **Scott Kemmerer**

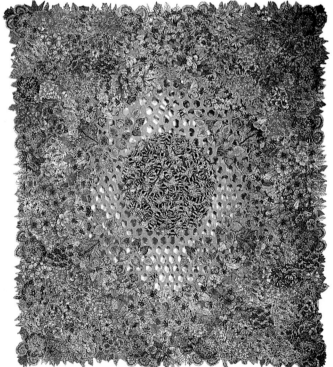

M. Joan's process is a complex one—starting with her hand-dyed fabrics. With photo emulsion screen prints she created her flowers in a variety of hues. After heat setting them, the flowers were hand-painted with markers and paints, and were cut out individually or in small clusters. Each was zigzag stitched around the edges and stuffed. Leaves were made the same way, and all were hand-painted with patterns of tiny dots. Flowers were stitched or tacked in place, and some leaves were secured with a vein pattern. The center panel was hand-painted a honey yellow before the hexagons were drawn, zigzag stitched, and cut away, leaving openings in the fabric. The central area was made up of individually printed, painted, and stuffed bees stitched to the backing.

Mary Lou Pepe
Colors of High Resolve, 60" x 102"
photo: Carina Woolrich

On the 75th anniversary of Woman's Suffrage, Mary Lou created this panel to commemorate the struggles of early suffragists. Using historical photographs, she enlarged and copied them onto clear acetate or special architect's vellum. From these she made photo emulsion screens to print the figures on her hand-dyed fabrics. The script (a quote from President Wilson in 1917 and used by the suffragists when they picketed the White House) was typed into the computer, printed out on vellum, and exposed on the photo emulsion screen. The fifty stars in the quilt center are couched with pearl cotton, while ribbons are used for the stripes. The forty-eight stars in the upper left represent the forty-eight states in the Union at the time of ratification.

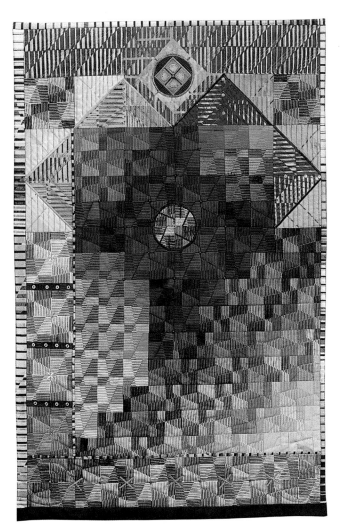

Karen N. Soma
Barricade, 37" x 24½"
photo: Roger Schreiber

The process which Karen used in this panel involves the use of copiers to develop and repeat her drawing motifs. Once the design was decided on, she prepared a photo silk-screen, using Hunt Speedball Emulsion, and printed on fabric which she had dyed or painted with fiber reactive dyes. Karen printed and overprinted, with Unidye™, adding a variety of metallics and pearlescents. The resulting images, mostly 4" modules, were then cut apart, pieced, layered and stitched, machine quilted, and embellished for a highly enriched and complex surface.

Jane Dunnewold
Beth's Magic Carpet, 90" x 46"
photo: Jane Dunnewold

Jane's screen-printed panel is
worked in horizontal bands on
her hand-painted background
fabrics. The artist, who wrote
Complex Cloth, printed black
images, then spray painted the
whole thing with white textile
paint, softening and graying the
contrast. The speckled pattern
at the bottom of the panel
resulted when black beads, sewn
to the panel, picked up the
white spray paint.

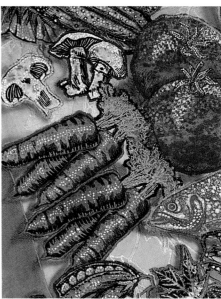

M. Joan Lintault
Give Us This Day, 5' 9" x 5' 3"
Detail of *Give Us This Day*
photo: Dan Overturf

After machine stitching the lace-
like tablecloth (in itself a remarkable feat), M. Joan screen printed
a grand array of fruits, vegetables,
and fish to cover the side panels
of the cloth. The technique used is
similar to that of *When The Bee
Stings*, page 96.

Karen N. Soma
Midnight Passage, 36" x 30"
photo: Roger Schreiber

Karen's color gradations are developed in part from the twenty or more dyed fabrics in each panel, used in combination with repeated over-prints. Her basic designs can be combined and re-combined to produce endless variations. This panel shows the complexity of her approach.

Jane Dunnewold
Pleasure Principle #3, 24" x 24"
photo: Jane Dunnewold

After painting her background fabrics with Deka silk paints, Jane used photo emulsion screen printing to add patterns and textures. The vertical, overlapping shape in red was painted on interfacing, then appliquéd to the panel. Foils were used to create the brilliant squares which were fused to the panel. Hand-painted interfacing (a non-fraying material) was used to create the irregular sawtoothed border of overlapping layers.

A small-format <u>positive</u> (slide) can be projected and enlarged directly onto a sensitized screen in the direct emulsion process. Either oil-based or water-based paints can be used for printing. You will need projection and darkroom equipment for this method and will find materials at any large photographic supply house. All steps are identical with the process for photo emulsion screening except that exposure occurs in the darkroom, not outside. Exposure times are given with the specific emulsion being used.

THERMAL IMAGERS (COPIERS)

Thermal imaging, a process known to many teachers, is a sure-fire and easy way to add <u>lettering</u>, photographs, sketches, or linear designs to cloth without the use of chemicals, solvents, or knives. Designs or photos are etched or burned onto a special plastic film (the thermal screen) in the <u>thermal imager</u>. This film or stencil is attached to a plastic frame for screen-printing. The screen can be saved and re-used.

In addition to thermal imagers, there is the similar Print Gocco. Thermo-Fax exposes with a quartz light; Print Gocco uses a flashbulb, but the principle is similar. Designed in Japan as a toy for children, Print Gocco was made for use on paper. One drawback has been the limited area for printing, but there is now an attachable handle for stamping as well as a removable printing plate, making it easier to print on large surfaces. It requires the use of its own brand of paints for stamping. Both Print Gocco and Thermo-Fax offer easy alternatives to photo emulsion.

As trucks deliver new copy machines and computers to schools all over the country, the older thermal imagers are often put into retirement. Once used in schools and offices to produce stencils or spirit masters for dittos, few remain in use. Fabric artists now prize them for creating photographic stencils.

Although thermal imagers are still being made, old ones can often be purchased very reasonably. My somewhat ancient machine, purchased from a less ancient retired schoolteacher, was one of my wiser investments. Place want ads, check with school equipment suppliers, or call your school district for auction dates. If you work in a school or office which has a thermal imager, for heaven's sake, try it out. Welsh Co., a supplier of screens, also sells new and refurbished thermal imagers. Most were manufactured by 3M as Thermo-Fax, Secretary, or Transparency Makers, but Apollo also made a brand, and all will image the screens.

Jan L. Boyer
Giverny
Detail of *Giverny*
photo: David Gratz

Inspired by a trip to Monet's gardens, Jan first painted her fabric with Procion MX using a watercolor technique. Over that she Thermofaxed motifs which reminded her of the overflowing gardens.

thermo-fax printing

Once you are familiar with the simple thermal-screen printing process, it is just minutes from drawing to print. You need no wood frame, no emulsion, and the screens can be saved for re-use. I have yet to wear out a thermal screen. Since thermal screens produce good details and lettering, they are great for labels, name tags, and text on fabric. The imager works best on linear designs and will not always print large open areas.

WHAT YOU NEED

Basic silk-screen supplies
(page 70)
Copy of original
Access to thermal imager
Thermal screen (mesh)
Plastic mat or frame
Double-faced tape

THE PROCESS

1. Place a copy of your original face up, under the mesh, and on top of a carrier.
2. Expose it by inserting the three layers (carrier, copy, and mesh) into the machine.
3. Set the imager to medium and press the "on" button. The layers will be drawn through the machine and will emerge with the design burned onto the surface of the screen.
4. Carefully peel the mesh away from the copy.
5. Adhere double-faced tape to all four inside edges of a plastic frame. See illustration below.
6. Attach the mesh to a frame by pressing it onto the tape. The shiny surface of the mesh should be down and in contact with the frame. Keep the screen taut (but not bowed).
7. Place fabric on a flat, smooth surface.
8. Place the frame over the fabric. Print.

Original

Any original must be photocopied or black and white laser printed, as the heat in the thermal imager responds to carbon. A carbon pencil or India ink will work, but most pencils, ballpoint pens, and felt markers have inadequate carbon to image clearly. Press-on letters, snapshots, signatures, and paste-ups must all be photocopied.

Thermal Screens or Stencils

Thermal screens (the mesh) consist of two adhered layers. A finely woven polyester fabric is bonded with a thin plastic film. When the screen (or mesh) is placed over a copy and run through the imager, the copy is etched into the plastic but not through the fabric of the mesh. This creates a stencil.

Thermal screens are available in pre-cut sheets or by the roll, which is less expensive per print, but has a higher initial cost. You will be limited in size only by the page-size capacity of the thermal imager (8½" x 11"). You can run a longer sheet through, but not a wider one.

Carrier

To keep the layers together as they are imaged, use a carrier. A piece of copy paper will do. Fold one end over by an inch and crease sharply. The copy and the mesh can be slipped into that fold. Some screens come with a backing sheet attached, so no other carrier is needed.

Imaging

You need three layers to expose or image your screen: the carrier, the copy, and the thermal screen. Place the screen, mesh side up and shiny side down, on top of the carrier and slip your copy in between. Your design must allow space at the edges of the frame for a "well."

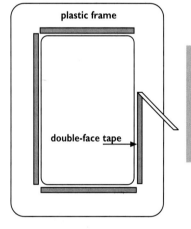

plastic frame

double-face tape

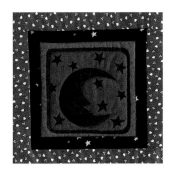

When making your first thermal image, set the adjustable dial just past the midway point, going towards dark. After running your screen through, carefully lift a corner to check the stencil. The design should be etched into the screen so you can see light through the open areas. If the design does not show, it was inadequately exposed, and the sandwich can be run through again at a slightly longer setting. If the design was overexposed the screen will stick to the original. Experiment to determine the perfect setting. Mark that spot on the dial. The control dial does not change the temperature, but rather alters speed. A slower speed allows for a longer exposure to the heat.

Print Frame

In contrast to the sturdy wood of a silk-screen frame, this method uses a lightweight, easily cleaned, re-usable plastic frame which holds the screen taut and makes it easier to handle. Larger frames (for 8$\frac{1}{2}$" x 11") can be handled after some practice, but half-size frames are easy, and the smallest size will be a snap. Plastic frames are convenient, but in a pinch you can make one out of cardboard. Cut a window in a letter-sized sheet of smooth cardboard. The window should be one inch smaller than the size of the mesh. After imaging, attach the mesh to the frame.

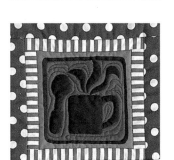

To do this, apply double-faced tape to the inside edges of the plastic frame, see page 101. Place mesh on top and press into place. (It will tend to curl down or under.) Mesh should be smooth and free of wrinkles.

Screening

Always run a test print on paper. Spoon a small amount of <u>textile paint</u> onto an unimaged area. Draw the squeegee lightly but firmly, pulling paint across the image. Lift the screen carefully off the fabric, and let the fabric dry. (See Screening Techniques on pages 69-70.)

Clean-up

Remove excess paint from the screen, using the squeegee as a scoop. Unmixed paint can go back into the jar. Place the screen over newspaper or paper towels, and wipe off remaining paint. Wash both screen and frame under cool to lukewarm water. Dry with paper towels. The design (mesh) can be kept on the frame and stored that way for further use. Or, the mesh can be carefully removed for later re-use. Occasionally the mesh will tear as it is removed and must be discarded.

Betsy Cosart
Detail of *RVs*

Betsy Cosart adapted simple drawings to get the RVs, motor homes, fifth wheelers, and a dinghy caravaning down the highway. She printed them using Thermo-Fax and added bright colors with hand painting and freezer-paper stencils. Silver metallic added a reflective touch to hub caps and bumpers.

Storing

Keep unused, unexposed screens in a dust-free area (the box they come in will do nicely). Store away from direct sunlight and heat. In hot weather, keep them in an air-conditioned room.

After exposure or imaging, light is not a problem. Stack frames vertically. If mesh has been removed from the frame, store the screen in a manila folder.

Multicolored Prints

A print of two or more colors can be made in any of several ways. First, you can separate the colors of your original. If you have a picture of a redhead wearing a blue hat, one screen can be for the red and one for blue. You image each color on its own screen, using any of several <u>registration</u> methods.

Or image both the redhead and her blue hat on one screen, then block off either the red or blue area. Make a print on paper. From the paper print, cut out only the area of the blue hat. The paper print becomes a <u>stencil</u> or <u>block-out</u>. Place it under the screen, align it with the stencil, and tape the edge to the frame. Print the blue color, then follow the same process for the second color by making a different paper print from which a stencil can be cut. It will cover the area of the hat and open the area for the redhead. This is difficult where precise registration is needed; don't count on getting the pupils into the middle of the eyes. But it's relatively simple for shapes which do not have to fit precisely, such as the stem on a flower.

It is also possible, with some careful maneuvering, to use several colors of paint at one time. You'll need a small plastic squeegee for each color (just 1" or 2" lengths will do). Put a small amount of each color on the screen near the area to be printed in that color. Go over each area with a separate color and squeegee. Try to keep one color from invading another's territory. When parts of the design are separated, this will work easily. For example, three stars spaced on one screen can be printed in three different colors.

A rainbow effect can be screened if you spoon various colors, one after another, at one end of the screen. Squeegee across with one stroke to get a rainbow effect; no two prints will be identical. They'll eventually blend and you'll have to start over to retain the effect. Always squeegee in the same direction to keep colors from mixing.

TROUBLESHOOTING FOR THERMAL IMAGING

Problem: The print is smeared, or the paint appears to have run.
Solution: Stencil may be overexposed. Readjust the heat control.
             There is too much paint. Squeegee with less pressure, and hold squeegee more upright.
             Frame may have moved during printing.
Problem: The print appears light and sketchy, or parts of it are lost.
Solution: Stencil may be underdeveloped. Try again at a higher setting.
             Too little paint was used. Squeegee with more pressure, and hold squeegee more parallel to screen.
Problem: Pinhole spots of paint appear on the fabric where it should be clear.
Solution: Mask leaks with cellophane tape on the underside of the screen.
             Clean belt or roller with alcohol.
             Make sure copy is clean. Dust particles will etch.
Problem: Mesh tears when separated from the copy after exposure.
Solution: Overexposed. Use less heat to image the design.

Dish Towels

Computer lettering printouts were cut-and-pasted to create the arches. A photocopy was then made so that drawings and lettering could all be thermal screened.

Jody House
Mother Jones, 32¹/₂" x 32¹/₂"

A portrait of labor leader Mother Jones dominates the center of this quilt which celebrates her politically active life. Jody quoted Mother Jones in the border of her thermal screened piece.

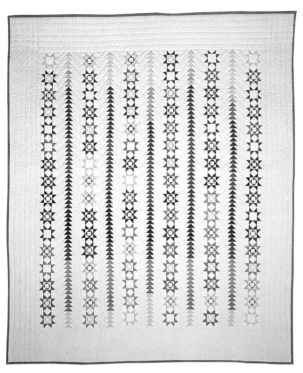

Jody House
Rainbow Quilt, 62" x 52"

Each eight-pointed star of this pristine traditional quilt pattern was thermal screened individually. Each smaller square-in-a-square was printed within the larger star. All were pieced to make the long rows of clear, bright stars. Flying geese printed four at a time were joined the same way.

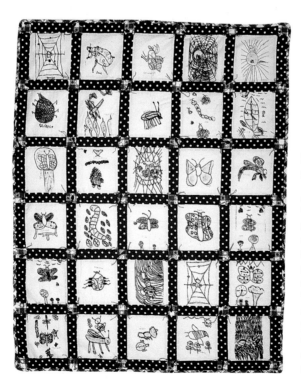

Kathy Miller
Backyard Monster Quilt, 54" x 45"

After a museum excursion to see "backyard monsters," each student in Kathy's second-grade class drew a favorite bug. These were copied, imaged, and thermal screened by the students on pre-cut fabric with Versatex paints. The assembled quilt is alive with creepy-crawlers—to the great pleasure of the students. It is tied with red cords, and stamp printed on the back is the name of the school, the class, and the date.

Jean Ray Laury
Yosemite Bank Quilt, 126" x 90"
quilted by Susan Smeltzer
Detail of *Yosemite Bank Quilt*
photo: Sharon Risedorph

Using the local flora and fauna for
inspiration, this large panel,
comissioned for a new bank in
Oakhurst, California, was
Thermo-Fax printed. Many of the
images were fragmented and
reassembled, then hand-colored
with thinned Versatex. The quilting lines enhance the shapes, as
seen on the block of Half Dome.

Frances R. MacEachren
Cooling Towers, 44" x 44"
photo: Richard E. Ackley

Fran photocopied her sketches of
skeletons and created a screen
for thermal imaging. These prints
were then combined with pieced
elements in *Cooling Towers*.

Jean Ray Laury
Vests and detail

Thermal printed fabrics in
stripes, checks, and herbs, each
printed in a different color range,
were pieced for the ten vests
made for waiters in a local
restaurant.

Jean Ray Laury
Nineteen, 40" x 30"
photo: Sharon Risedorph

Nineteen, a commemorative quilt for Oklahoma City, was printed from Thermo-Fax screens. Small areas were hand colored with thinned Versatex.

Patricia Malarcher
Detail of *Locolibrium*
photo: D. James Dee

Patricia copied her own drawings and doodles on a black and white laser printer for exposure in the Gocco Printer. She printed with black paint, applying the designs over painted canvas. All squares were finally sewn to heavy artist's linen.

Print Gocco

Print Gocco is a <u>thermal imager</u> which creates a screen by exposure of the design and mesh to flashbulb. The design is burned or etched into the plastic of a mesh screen, leaving open areas, or a <u>stencil</u>, for printing. The process is similar to thermal imaging and it greatly simplifies the creation of photo screens.

There is a separate stamping kit which can be removed from the printer to allow for work on larger areas or on yardage. Special inks must be used. Prints can be multicolored. The basic printer costs about $120, plus bulbs and screen, but it is a tremendous time saver. Specific directions are not given here, since they come with the Print Gocco.

CHAPTER 6

light-sensitive printing

Fabric artists with an inclination toward sleight of hand will particularly enjoy the four methods described in this section. It is exciting to see images emerge, somewhat magically, on exposed fabric. Watching your great-uncle materialize on cloth will transform you into an eager alchemist. The methods covered in this chapter include:

cyanotype or blueprint
van dyke or brownprint
kwik-print
inko print

These photo processes involve the use of sensitized fabrics which, upon exposure to ultraviolet light, develop their full color. You've experienced this kind of exposure in a swimsuit on a summer day. The next day, stripped, you appear to be wearing a flesh-colored suit, while areas exposed to the sun are "fully developed" in red. This is essentially the process utilized in all four methods. A block-out or negative, placed in direct contact with the fabric, interrupts the light in the same way that your swimsuit interrupted the tan. This is a contact print.

All light-sensitive processes are particularly inviting because of the quality of the images they produce. Fabric photographs from halftone negatives are richly detailed, and natural forms give a characteristic variation of intensity. A photographic negative used on sensitized fabric produces a positive photographic image. Those areas which look dark on a negative will inhibit the flow of light and preserve the original fabric color. An opaque object or block-out, as opposed to a photo negative, produces a photogram.

WARNING: Sensitizers (or light-sensitive chemicals) are toxic, so they must be handled and stored with extreme caution. Use pre-mixed liquids when possible. If you must mix dry ingredients, wear neoprene gloves and a long-sleeved shirt. Wear a mask and goggles and work outdoors with a safe-box or with a hooded vent. Leave your cup of coffee (and your cigar) out in the kitchen, and no children or open flames near the solutions. Read the <u>Hazardous Materials</u> entry in Additional Help. To avoid handling chemicals, purchase fabrics already prepared for exposure or buy ready-mixed liquids. Read about these on pages 113 and 122.

The following step-by-step directions apply to the mixing and applying of chemicals. Restrain yourself and hold still long enough to read this entire section before proceeding to the specific method that has you intrigued.

GENERAL INFORMATION

Before starting, collect your materials. (Utensils should be reserved exclusively for this work.)

WHAT YOU NEED	THE PROCESS
Light-sensitive solution	1. Put on neoprene gloves and face mask to mix chemicals.
Small glass bowls (for mixing and painting)	
Brown or amber bottles for storing solutions	2. Coat fabric with light-sensitive solution.
Plastic mixing spoons	3. Dry in a darkroom.
Gram or ounce scale	4. Place sensitized fabric on the base of the direct-contact frame (see page 112).
Neoprene gloves	
Face mask	5. Place negative or block-out on the fabric. Cover with glass.
Safe-box	
Two sheets of Plexiglas or <u>glass</u> (one on which to paint the fabric, one for the contact frame)	6. Expose to sunlight or artificial light to develop.
<u>Direct-contact frame</u>	7. Rinse fabric, set, and dry.
<u>Darkroom</u> with safe-light	
Paint brush or sponge brush	
Plastic clothesline (to dry fabric)	
Fabric, cut slightly smaller than the glass	

SOURCE LIST

<u>Cyanotype</u> chemicals, 25, 29

Face mask, 5, 21 22

<u>Inkodye</u>, 1, 35

<u>Kwik-Print</u>, 32

Neoprene gloves, 5, 19

<u>Van Dyke</u> chemicals, 32

Darkroom

To produce clear images, you must prevent light exposure during application, drying, and preparation of the sensitizer; though there is some leeway. You have a few minutes in which to work in subdued light, or with a safe-light. Drying requires darkness, since it takes the longest time. Working at night eases darkroom concerns, and "night people" prefer this. Their fabrics are then ready for printing at sun-up, even if they're not.

CAUTION: Do not perform this work in your kitchen. If you have no darkroom, use a bathroom, laundry room, or work at night and cover the dry sensitized fabric before daylight hits it. Wash the work areas thoroughly.

For light-sensitive methods, your darkroom will need a plastic clothesline on which to dry the fabric. Unless you have concrete floors and absolutely no qualms about how they look, you'll need to protect the floor under the drying area. Use a sheet of plastic with newspapers spread over it. (Take care not to go into a banana-peel routine by slipping on the plastic.) If you use a bathroom, hang a line over the tub (with a travel clothesline or suction cups). Line it with newspaper, or add an inch or two of water to catch any drips and make cleaning easier. When working with a single piece of fabric, let it dry on a sheet of Plexiglas.

Sensitizing Solutions

To avoid mixing dry chemicals, use pre-treated fabric for cyanotype and purchase the ready-mixed liquids for Kwik-Print and Inko prints. All light-sensitive solutions have limited shelf lives, and solutions or pre-coated fabrics will have an expiration date. Mixing the chemicals yourself, although more hazardous, assures their viability.

Most chemicals needed for light-sensitive prints are available through photographic, scientific, or craft suppliers. Carefully estimate the amount of solution needed, to avoid having problems of <u>disposal</u>. Just 4 tablespoons of solution will coat from one to three page-sized pieces of fabric, so don't buy pounds of it. The specific amount used will be determined in part by the weight of the fabric and the degree of fabric saturation. Caution must be taken in the care and storage of these materials, and it is safer to keep only a minimum amount on hand.

Reserve all bottles, bowls, and tools for light-sensitive solutions only. Do not re-use them to feed the cat or to mix paint, and never let them find their way back to the kitchen. A strip of red tape will readily identify them as off-limits for other uses.

Always clean work areas with sudsy water after you have finished.

Keep materials in a locked cupboard where children have no access to them. Do not allow small children in your work area.

Safe-Box

If you choose to mix your chemicals, a safe-box similar to one used in medical labs is recommended. These are available through medical supply houses or chemical labs. They consist of a Plexiglas-topped box with hand holes at the sides fitted with neoprene gloves. All chemicals are used inside the box, protecting you from breezes (or sneezes) or spills.

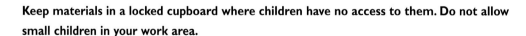

Negatives

The print you make will be the same size as the negative you use. For a larger print, you'll need a larger negative. Negatives can be made from any <u>positive transparency</u> (slide), photograph, print, or tintype. Check with local photo labs, as prices vary considerably. Negatives with strong contrast give the clearest images on fabric. Ask for <u>halftone negatives</u>. Store your negatives carefully to avoid scratches, as they can be used over and over.

To embellish a photo, place your photo negative on a sheet of white paper or over a light table, so you can see the image. Then place a transparent sheet (an acetate) over the negative and add your drawing to it. In this way you could place a halo over your own head, or sketch smoke coming out of your brother's ears, without damaging your negative. The two transparencies (the negative plus your acetate drawing) are stacked and exposed simultaneously. By removing the acetate with the drawing part-way through the exposure time, you could give the drawing a shadowy effect.

Drawings and Words

You will need a block-out of opaque letters on a transparency to print words. You can apply self-adhesive letters directly to acetate or glass. Even marking-pen letters on plastic bags will work, but it is more difficult to manage a flexible surface than a rigid sheet. Drawings of words can be copied onto a transparency, but the lines must be opaque enough to inhibit light. Photocopy and re-draw lines that appear too sketchy or faint, adjust the copier for a darker print, or use a printer and adjust the print density.

Contact Prints

All light-sensitive methods involve contact prints. The flatter the object, the better the contact. The more light eliminated, the clearer the print will be. A flat leaf works well. But a pine cone will give fuzzy images where light slips under the spines. Paper <u>cut-outs</u>, ferns, silverware, anything that will cast a shadow, will give a print. If you are printing your great-grandmother's photograph, consider including a print of her gloves, a pressed rose, or her comb. Tools of trades and hobbies can enhance the personal character of a piece. A stethoscope, calipers, eyeglasses, or pocket knife may convey a more complete portrait than the photograph alone.

When objects are not pressed flat in a <u>contact frame</u>, gradations of color may be printed. A branch, for example, will let light pass where leaves are slightly curved. A bump or breeze, which moves your <u>block-out</u>, may make a double print, but you can also move objects deliberately for shadowy effects. If you are not using glass, pin any leaves, negatives, or other lightweight pieces in place. Cut fabrics 1" to 2" larger than your design.

Textures

Textures and patterns can serve as unifying elements in prints. Metal or plastic screens of various sizes produce linear checks. Dotted nets add delicate patterns. Scattering rice, confetti, spaghetti, or dried peas directly on fabric adds overall texture or pattern. Flexible wire or strings can be used to create drawings. If this is too undisciplined for your way of working, arrange the objects on a copier, make a transparency, and use it over negatives or other block-outs.

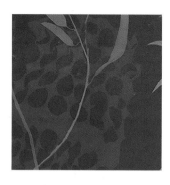

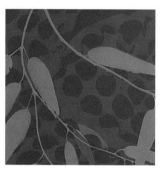

Ultraviolet Light

All light-sensitive contact exposures require ultraviolet light. Ultraviolet bulbs are expensive and exposure times vary, so do a test piece. Mercury vapor or sun lamps require special precautions. You must protect yourself from sunburn (UV sunglasses, gloves, long sleeves). Never use a carbon arc light as your light source. I recommend you wait for a sunny day, since sunshine provides the best and safest source.

If, however, rain interferes and you are impatient, a sunlamp (GE Sunlamp UV®) will work on dry treated fabric. The light source must be at a distance sufficient to give an overall, even exposure and to avoid hot spots. A general rule for this distance is $1\frac{1}{2}$ times the diagonal measurement of your print area. Exposure time is 30-40 minutes.

Fabric

Each light-sensitive method is best suited to specific fabrics. Check the Work Chart on pages 6-7. Cut fabrics to size, 1" to 2" larger than your negatives or transparencies, but not larger than the glass on which you will print them. Or to expose larger fabric pieces, select objects that won't move and don't need glass to hold them. Pin them in place, or plan on movement (blurred or shadow-like images) in the design. The edge of the glass will refract the light and imprint that line on the fabric.

Sensitizing the Fabric

Mix the sensitizing ingredients according to the instructions. Note precautions on page 109. Smooth the fabric onto a sheet of glass and paint the fabric with the chemical solution. If you are sensitizing only one piece of fabric, let it dry on the glass. For several, carefully lift the painted fabric by the corners and hang it to dry in a darkroom. As the fabric is now light-sensitive, no light should reach it. Wash your hands thoroughly (also wash the gloves), and go have a cup of coffee. Or several cups. You could even go out and buy a pound of coffee beans, as it will take the fabric a while to dry. Warm air and a fan will speed up the drying.

Exposure

Stack the direct contact frame with the design (transparency, negative, <u>natural forms</u>, or whatever) on top of the fabric. Use photo negatives shiny side up (so they look "right"). Place a sheet of clean glass over the top (not the one you painted on, as it will have sensitizer on it). This makes a sandwich, as shown in the illustration below. The glass holds the layers flat, assuring good contact. It also holds in place any lightweight leaves, feathers, lace, or paper cut-outs which might otherwise shift or disappear entirely with a slight breeze, and transparencies, which might curl in the sun. On a perfectly still day, rice or leaves placed on the fabric would stay put without the glass.

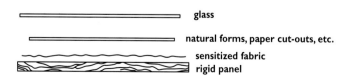

glass

natural forms, paper cut-outs, etc.

sensitized fabric
rigid panel

Once the materials sandwich is ready, place it out in direct bright sunlight perpendicular to the sun's rays. Time will vary with the time of day, temperature (65° to 70° is ideal), time of year, clarity of the air, and the process used, ranging from 5 to 30 minutes. (On a clear summer day a 5 minute exposure should be adequate.) With practice you will get a feel for the right timing. The changing color of the fabric is your best guide. If the sun goes under a cloud, you'll have to increase exposure time. Results are most predictable and colors are brighter with full sunlight.

Oversize Pieces

One method for printing larger fabrics is to expose the fabric while it is wet. This means that no glass will be placed over the top. A wet exposure avoids the problem of drying the sensitized fabric. Use a smooth surface under the fabric, such as foamcore or a foil-covered board. For garments, the pattern parts can be cut and exposed individually before assembly. Consider making large panels in sections. Barbara Hewitt uses 4' x 8' insulated board covered with foil and butcher paper for her large pieces.

Ritva

A photo negative was used as the block-out for this cyanotype.

CYANOTYPE OR BLUEPRINT

Cyanotype (Greek for blueprint) takes its name from the color of the finished prints, which ranges from a light blue-green to deep blue. This is the most popular and familiar of the light-sensitive methods. The process is similar to blueprint on paper: areas protected from exposure retain the original fabric color, while exposed areas develop to blue.

Cyanotype works best on natural PFP fabrics: cotton, linen, or silk. Chintz and sateen give soft images, flannel gives a rich, deep color. Muslin, with its yellowish cast, turns prints greenish. Silk details beautifully.

ready-to-go blueprint

Pre-treated fabrics, available in squares (perfect for quilt blocks) or in yardage, offer a great way to get acquainted with this process. Blueprint chemicals are pre-applied to magenta, white, or turquoise backgrounds. (Yes, like green oranges, we now have magenta blueprints.) These pre-treated materials preclude the mixing of chemicals, simplify the process, and are safe. No warning of chronic toxicity is required for these products. Exposure by ingestion or inhalation is unlikely, but always scrub hands thoroughly after handling fabrics.

To expose pre-treated fabrics, follow directions for exposure on pages 112-113. (Instructions also come with the fabrics.) Remove fabrics from their lightfast packets away from bright light only when you are ready to expose them.

SOURCE LIST

Pre-treated blueprint fabric, 14, 25

Norma Wooddell
Fern

Ferns provided the block-out for this small blueprint panel exposed under glass.

preparing YOUR OWN blueprint

See <u>Sensitizers</u> and <u>Hazardous Materials</u> in Additional Help. While cyanotype is considered to be only "slightly toxic," it is important to wear neoprene gloves and a face mask. To order chemicals listed in the following recipe, see Source List on page 109. You may wish to cut the recipe in half for a trial run. Prepare the following in the safe-box:

Solution A: Dissolve
2 ounces (60 grams) of ferric ammonium citrate in
8 ounces (1 cup or 250 ml) of distilled water, using a small glass bowl and a plastic mixing spoon.

Solution B: Dissolve
1 ounce (30 grams) of potassium ferricyanide in
8 ounces (1 cup or 250 ml) of distilled water, using a second small glass bowl and plastic mixing spoon.

Solution C (in a darkroom):
Combine Solutions A and B. The mixture is now light-sensitive.

Solutions A and B should be kept in separate amber or brown bottles, to be mixed together in equal amounts just before using. If you are really enthusiastic and make cyanotype prints frequently, one artist suggests that you keep adding to the same container; store any leftover mixture in a brown bottle in a dark place to prevent exposure. The next time you print, add equal additional amounts of mixtures A and B to the remaining mixture C. Other artists recommend using the mixture within six hours. Obviously, there is some flexibility there! Stored separately, the mixed chemicals have a shelf life up to six months. (Dry chemicals can be kept indefinitely.)

In the <u>darkroom</u>, paint your fabric directly from the bowl in which you mixed. Half of the recipe, a total of one cup, is ample for many cyanotype prints.

When the fabric is dry, place it over the direct contact frame with the <u>negative</u>, then <u>glass</u> on top. See illustration below. Put the stack in direct bright sunlight. The exposure time will vary from 5 to 30 minutes. When the material turns a charcoal blue, remove it from the sunlight.

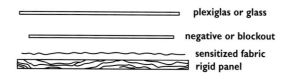

plexiglas or glass

negative or blockout

sensitized fabric

rigid panel

Blue-printing a T-shirt is not a project for the beginner, who would be better off purchasing a pre-treated shirt or making smaller prints which could be sewn onto a shirt. If you must try it, stretch the fabric over a rigid surface (foamcore or covered cardboard) and expose one side. Then turn it over and expose the second side before rinsing.

Rinsing and Care

After exposure, the blueprint must be thoroughly rinsed. Wear neoprene gloves to rinse by hand or (for larger pieces) use a washing machine. If you have hard water, use distilled or bottled water for the final rinse. To hand wash cyanotypes and <u>Van Dyke</u> prints, use $\frac{1}{2}$ teaspoon of mild dishwashing liquid per gallon of cool water. Too much soap, or soap used directly on the print, will cause fading. Never use any product that contains phosphates or bleaching agents (chlorine, borax, or soda). These products will turn the brilliant blues to yellow. While the prints are washable, some artists maintain that color brilliance is lost in washing, and they limit their work to wallhangings or panels. Others claim permanence. Because of these variables in the process, test prints are important.

Cyanotype prints can be dry-cleaned. When exposed to sunlight or continuous daylight, the colors will lighten. Giving them a rest in the dark restores the color.

Clean all work surfaces and the neoprene gloves with hot, soapy water. Discard any leftover chemical mixtures following manufacturer's recommendations and read <u>Disposal</u> in Additional Help. Label any unused chemicals clearly and keep them away from heat and light in a locked cupboard.

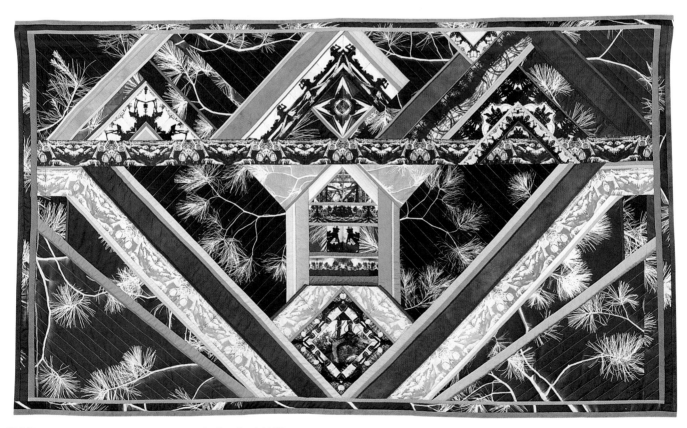

Tafi Brown
Tree Cycle, 42" x 72"
photo: Jeff Baird

Cyanotypes were exposed, printed, cut apart, and pieced in this intricate panel. Tafi paints her own fabrics for her blueprints, often making multiples of as many as four to eight. The geometric four-pointed star (upper center) was pieced from multiples of an organic shape. This is one of a series she is doing on trees; this one is based on the species from which her house was built.

Tafi Brown
Growing/Healing, 47" x 47"
photo: Tafi Brown

Growing/Healing was exposed
using student's hands directly on
the cloth. The 4th, 8th, and 12th
grader's handprints varied in
color due in part to changes in
the length of exposure time—
both how long the hand stayed
on the fabric and how long the
fabric was left exposed to
sunlight. The moisture on hands
also affected exposure, as did
unexpected rain showers.

Karen R. McKee
Dem Bones, 50" x 16"
photo: Paul Boyer

When Karen fell and shat-
tered an ankle several years
ago, a collection of x-rays
began to accumulate. There
were x-ray views of the break,
more of the inserted plate
and screws, and still more
when the plate was removed.
Because she had been working with cyanotype, the idea of
using these x-rays seemed a
logical next step. Getting
permission to use the x-rays
for non-medical purposes
required "maneuverings and
fast talking" on her part.
This panel chronicles from top
to bottom the break to its
healed state. It was given to
her doctor, who had learned
to quilt from his grandmother.

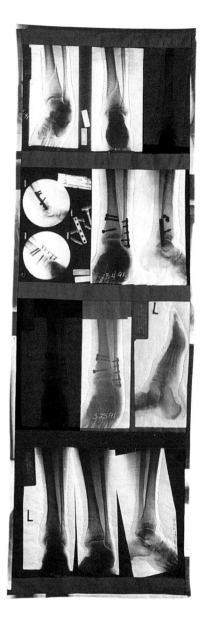

Karen R. McKee
Detail of *Fear of Falling*
photo: Paul Boyer

Karen gathered further documenta-
tion (hospital bills, Rx receipts,
wheelchair rental, insurance papers,
etc.). After enlarging and photocopying these onto acetate, she
cyanotyped them as shown in this
detail. The round surgery-room
x-rays were a great addition. The
quilt was tied with surgical thread,
and her "stitches" were added to
the blueprints. The experience
tended to demystify the whole
process for Karen. The images
became non-threatening and
instead of being "acted upon,"
she felt a greater control.

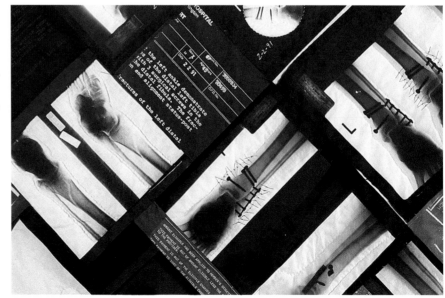

Barbara Hewitt
Blueprint Kimono, Blue

Barbara used a pink silk crepe in an exposure of four minutes (during summer in California) for this Kimono. A shorter exposure time creates a pastel effect in contrast to the deep, vibrant colors of a longer exposure. The leaves were pinned in place to prevent any movement and subsequent blurring.

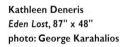

Barbara Hewitt
Blueprint Kimono, Red

Cyanotype, developed over red-orange charmeuse yardage produce a deep brown while protected areas retained the original fabric color. Barbara worked on a large foamcore panel and exposed the fabric for 15 minutes. She placed a piece of lightweight leather, from which silver-dollar sized holes had been punched, loosely over the fabric, and removed it after 12 minutes. Eucalyptus leaves remained in place the full 15 minutes.

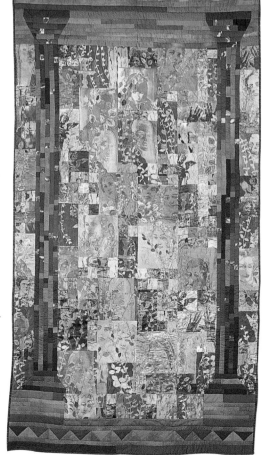

Kathleen Deneris
Eden Lost, 87" x 48"
photo: George Karahalios

To achieve an elusive and half-hidden effect, Kathleen used cyanotype to create the blocks in her *Eden Lost*. Faces seem to emerge, disappear, and re-emerge, as contrasting patterns and colors take over. Small bits of bright colored fabrics are stitched into place on the surface.

Brown Cast

To alter cyanotype to brown, or to rescue one that has turned yellow or is an uneven blue, dip the print into the following mixture. (The new color will never be more intense than the blue.) The recipe was suggested by Barbara Hewitt:

1. Dissolve 1 tablespoon TSP (trisodium phosphate) in hot water using a plastic bucket and plastic mixing spoon.
2. Add cold water to make 1 quart. This is enough for 2 or 3 small pieces of fabric. Save any excess for later use.
3. Soak the print until blue fades to yellow. (You will still see the image.)
4. Rinse under tap water.
5. Immerse 2 bags of Lipton's Tea (orange pekoe and pekoe-cut black) into 1 cup of boiling water.
6. Steep for 10 minutes to extract the tannic acid, then remove the tea bags. Add cool water.
7. Pour tea liquid into a flat container (a glass cake pan works well) and place the yellow print face side down. Soak for at least 30 minutes.
8. Yellow areas will turn brown. If the contrast is not strong enough, repeat the tea bath with a stronger solution.
9. Rinse well. Hang the fabric to dry. Solutions can be re-used.
10. Wash by hand. The color will not run or bleed, but may fade slightly. Press.

For a yellow and white print, follow steps 1 through 4 above. No tea; the yellow to gold tone depends on the color of the blueprint. For a violet cast, soak the blueprint in a cold borax solution. A brown tone can also be created by using a saturated solution of sodium bicarbonate (common baking soda) and tannic acid (from tea) in equal amounts, soaking fabric in the mixture to the desired color.

Erma Martin Yost
Woodland Spirit, 20" x 24"
photo: Leon Yost, Courtesy of
NoHo Gallery, SoHo NYC

Erma's *Woodland Spirit* evokes
the realm of birds, from the
limitless sky to the woodpecker's
shadowy form within the bird
house. The cloud patterns were
cyanotyped—the bird, dye
transferred. The pine needles
were printed from heat transfers
imaged on the color laser copier.
In the center area machine
embroidery was added for linear
detail and texture.

Erma Martin Yost
Dream Flight
each page 25" x 20" x 4"
photo: Leon Yost, Courtesy of
NoHo Gallery, SoHo NYC

Erma stitched transparent slices
of cloth against a cyanotype
background in *Dream Flight*.
Printed on these delicately
colored fabrics are lines of text,
each a dye transfer, in which disperse dye paper was transferred
to the toner of a black and white
copy, then heat transferred to
cloth. This book opens on a
center spine (a dowel, halved
lengthwise), to which the knitting
needles are attached through tiny
eye screws. The book's pages, rich
in white-on-white detail, turn on
the needles.

Jean Ritchie
Jacket

A combination of blueprinting
techniques combine in this
handsome jacket. A positive
transparency (not a negative) of
an elephant was used for the
clear, detailed image at lower left.
Contact paper letters on acetate
spelled out the word "elephant."
A definition, at right, was written
directly onto an acetate to
produce the light words on blue.
Prints of screens, grids, soap suds,
and grasses are inter-mixed.
The pre-treated squares were
exposed, then joined and sewn to
the fabric base, in this case a
cotton jacket. Larger pieces of
cyanotyped fabric were used for
bindings and set-in strips. Liquid
blueprint chemicals were painted
directly onto ribbing.

VAN DYKE OR BROWNPRINT

Except for the color difference, the Van Dyke process is similar to cyanotype. Prints range from deep rich brown to a light pale brown. The natural color gives a special added depth to portraits.

Follow the procedures for cyanotype. One manufacturer recommends mixing chemicals in a sink (easing clean-up), or use the safe-box.

In addition to adequate ventilation, a face mask or goggles and neoprene gloves are a must. Using pre-measured chemicals avoids handling and weighing. Avoid skin contact and inhalation and be particularly careful of your eyes. The resulting prints are stunning and will be worth all the care which must be taken. Mixtures of solutions 1 and 3 must be used with special care, as both are toxic and can cause burns.

Formulas vary from one company to another. Follow directions that come with the chemicals you buy. Some companies (Rockland, for example) sell chemicals already in solution. See Source List on page 109. If you purchase the chemicals separately, use the following recipe. You will need separate containers for mixtures 1, 2, and 3. They are not light-sensitive until combined.

Solution: 1: Dissolve
   3 ounces (90 grams) of ferric ammonium citrate (green) in
   8 ounces (1 cup or 250 ml.) of distilled water in a brown bottle.

Solution 2: Dissolve
   $\frac{1}{2}$ ounce (15 grams) of tartaric acid in
   8 ounces (1 cup or 250 ml.) of distilled water in a brown bottle.

Solution 3: Dissolve
   $1\frac{1}{4}$ ounces ($37\frac{1}{2}$ grams) of silver nitrate in
   8 ounces (1 cup or 250 ml.) of distilled water in a brown bottle.

Mixture:
   Add Solution 2 to Solution 1, stirring well. Slowly add Solution 3, stirring continuously. The final mixture will be 1 part each of Solutions 1+2, and 3. Try to estimate the amount you will need to avoid leftover chemicals.

The exposure process is identical to cyanotype, but the time is shorter.
   2 minutes exposure in full sunlight may be adequate.
   Rinse for 10 minutes.

The last step, which turns the image brown, is a final rinse in the hypo-clearing agent.
While the fabric is rinsing, mix the following:
   Hypo-Clearing Solution
   Dissolve:
   1 ounce of sodium thiosulfate in
   20 ounces of water.

Dip the rinsed print in the hypo-clearing agent for 15 seconds. When it turns brown, rinse in clear water for 15 to 20 minutes. Dry away from bright light. When dry, it may be ironed. Dispose of leftover chemicals by washing them down a drain with copious amounts of water. Never dispose of chemicals in a wastebasket!

Elia Woods
Home, 28" x 32"
photo: Jenny Woodruff

For *Home*, photographic negatives were blueprinted and then dipped in tannic acid to change them to a brown tone. Elia said she would now print them using Van Dyke for the brown tone, but this method was all she knew at the time. Other fabrics in the piece were discharge dyed.

Elia Woods
Oklahoma, 42" x 51½"
photo: Jenny Woodruff

Elia photographed historic documents, then used the negatives for her exposures. To create a border, she made numerous negatives of a single photograph, then flipped alternate ones, which she assembled so that many were printed on a single panel. Lettering was printed from her computer, enlarged on a copier, printed on a transparency, and used in the exposure.

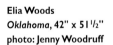

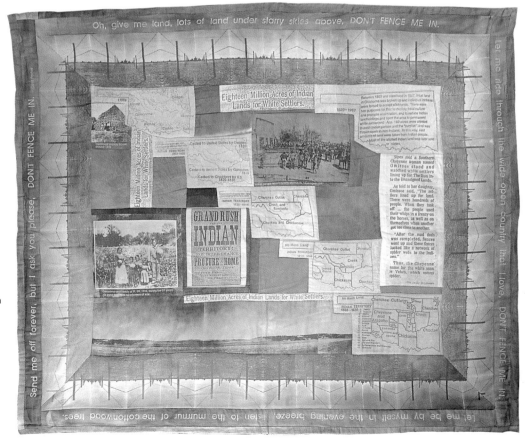

KWIK-PRINT

Kwik-Print does not require the mixing of any chemicals or dry powders. Pre-mixed emulsions consist of a light-sensitive solution in which colored pigments are held in suspension. This light-sensitive process has the advantage of a full range of colors that can be intermixed. Several different colors can be painted onto a single piece of fabric in a marbled, mottled, or striped effect.

Kwik-Print works best on synthetic fibers, especially acetate and polyesters. While it will print on cotton, silk, rayon, or blends, it may leave a slight residue in the light areas after rinsing. Exposure is faster than with cyanotype and varies from one color to another. Time may also depend on the density of the negative. A test piece is recommended.

The process is the same as for other light-sensitive methods without being limited to a single color. Its primary disadvantage is its higher cost. When Kwik-Print chemicals are purchased, specific directions will come with them. See Source List, page 109.

Follow the procedures given for cyanotype. Have fabrics well-pressed and prepare them for exposure in a darkroom. Brush on the Kwik-Print solution first in one direction, then at right angles to give thorough coverage. Solution color is identical to that of the finished print.

WARNING: Wear neoprene gloves, observe all precautions, and read all the information that accompanies the materials you buy. No food or drink and no children in the work area.

Here is a general guide for exposure:
Bright sunny day: 2 to 3 minutes
Gloomy day: up to 20 minutes
Sunlamp: (at 14" to 15") 8 to 15 minutes

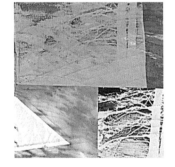

After exposure, rinse the fabric in cool water. Unexposed water-soluble chemicals will wash out and the image will begin to emerge. Add a few drops of liquid detergent to the surface to hasten removal of undeveloped pigment. Finally, rinse in the Fixing Solution.

Fixing Solution
Mix:
$\frac{1}{2}$ ounce of 28% ammonia in
1 gallon of hot water.
Rinse the print in the solution to fix it. Then rinse in clear water and iron dry. The finished Kwik-Print can be washed or dry-cleaned without affecting the printed image. It is colorfast and fade-resistant.

INKO PRINT

Inkodye (a vat dye) can be painted onto fabric to make it light-sensitive. Similar to Kwik-Print, it is available in a wide range of colors. The color develops as it is exposed to ultraviolet light. Pre-washed natural fabrics (cotton, linen, and rayon) work best for these contact prints. Inkodyes come in brown bottles for storage, and they have a shelf life of up to two years.

Since Inko comes in liquid form, no mixing or measuring is necessary. Care must be taken in handling the dyes.

Observe all precautions and read all manufacturer's warnings. Wear neoprene gloves and allow no food, drink, or children in the work area.

Working under subdued light, paint the Inkodyes onto fabric, following the directions given for cyanotype. Dry the fabric in a darkroom. Prepare a <u>direct contact frame</u> for exposure.

Approximate exposure time:
    10 minutes in sunlight, but varies from color to color.
    25 minutes under a sunlamp (at 14" to 15").
    Sunlight will give deeper and more brilliant colors.

After exposure, rinse in cold, soapy water until no further color rinses out. Dry on a flat surface. Iron on the reverse side of the print. Color will darken as it is ironed, and the dye will fume. Iron until all fuming ceases. The vapor given off during fuming is non-toxic, but it is sometimes irritating to the mucous membranes. Good ventilation and a face mask help, but ironing outdoors is best.

There will be some residue in the light areas, which varies from color to color. A white fabric, painted red, will have a reddish tinge in all the unexposed areas, since some color develops even without exposure to sunlight. If this seems unsatisfactory to you, switch to one of the other light-sensitive methods.

The wide range of colors available makes this a versatile process. As with Kwik-Print, you may paint several colors onto a fabric at one time. Inkodye is permanent to any kind of washing or cleaning. I once tried removing an Inkodye print by soaking it in a strong bleach solution, and the color never budged!

Nancy Halpern
Red Tide, 50" x 48½"
photo: **David Caras**

At top center Nancy's blueprint panel was exposed with fresh leaves as the block-out, producing white leaves on the colored ground. At the center bottom a red panel was exposed on wet Inko using seaweed and a plastic lobster. At center right a transparency of tree trunks was exposed on blueprint, giving sharp images in contrast to the same image used elsewhere on damp Inko, which is blurry. All were combined with hand-painted and shibori-dyed fabrics.

CHAPTER 7
stamp
printing

Stamps and Block Prints, Monoprints, Natural Forms, Embossing, and Foiling.

Anything which can be covered with paint and pressed to cloth provides a natural stamp or block print. Stamp printing is used effectively in grade B movies to show bloody handprints on white walls. Driver's license finger-printing or birth certificate footprints are stamp processes with which we're all familiar. Block prints transfer to cloth in the same way that muddy feet imprint floors. Monoprinting is a versatile method for inventive fabric printing. Nature provides an abundance of ready-to-use printing plates. All can be embellished with embossing or foiling. This chapter includes:

stamp and block prints

monoprints

natural forms

raised or metallic surfaces

STAMP AND BLOCK PRINTS

Anything that will pick up and transfer a layer of ink can be used as a stamp. Fingertips are a great start. While excellent commercially-made stamps abound, you may also want to make your own, which is at least half the fun.

The transition from stamp print to block print is primarily a matter of size. Stamps are inked on pads and hand pressed onto cloth. Blocks are inked with brayers or brushes and may require a press. The process of cutting or carving remains similar.

Although the term "rubber stamp" is often used, stamps and blocks are now made of many other materials. Like polyester silk-screens, we now have vinyl rubber stamps and plastic metallics.

WHAT YOU NEED

Stamps

Stamp pad

Inks or <u>textile paints</u>

<u>PFP fabric</u>

Iron and board

Brayer, brush, or markers (optional)

THE PROCESS

1. Coat the stamp with paint or ink—by means of pad, marker, brush, or <u>brayer</u>.
2. Press the inked stamp onto fabric, using some pressure.
3. Lift the stamp carefully, and let the fabric dry.
4. Heat set the print, if appropriate.

SOURCE LIST

Brayers, 1, 3, 19, 22, 34

Ink for fabric, 3, 8, 19, 21, 34

Stamp pads, 1, 3, 6, 8

ready-made stamps

Thousands of funny and wonderful stamps are available through mail-order catalogs and in stamp shops. The possibilities are as limitless as any stamper's imagination. There are wonderful books, organizations, and magazines, offering inspiration and information on exhibitions. It's another whole world.

Alphabet stamps vary greatly in size, font, and price. Check toy stores, airport gift shops, garage sales, and thrift stores. Some printing companies carry alphabets, and most stamp shops will have a good variety. Sponge alphabets and animal cut-outs are available in toy stores.

Deeply-etched stamps work best on fabric. Shallow cuts, fine for paper, are less satisfactory on the soft surface of cloth, since fibers may wick ink into the design.

Stamps can be made from your own designs. Check the yellow pages for ads and compare prices and sizes. You'll need camera-ready artwork, meaning it must look exactly as you want it to print, and must be in black and white. Most companies can do a <u>reversal</u> of your work. Photographs, lettering, and drawings can all be laser-cut into a flexible plastic material, then mounted on acrylic blocks. It is more expensive to have custom stamps made, but it is also more fun.

Stamp Pads

Stamp pads can be purchased or improvised, but all need to absorb and retain ink on a level surface so that ink can be picked up on a stamp. Commercial pads in lidded tin boxes work fine and retain their moisture well. Some stamp pads contain pigments and come in a wide range of colors. You can also purchase uninked pads from stamp shops and add your own textile color. Store stamp pads upside down so the ink will be at the surface when you use them.

CHAPTER 7

Inks

You can stamp your fabrics with any permanent ink, such as Carter's® (purple or black) or Sanford's (black). The bright colored IMPRINTZ™ and Pelikan inks are permanent and, being thin, print finer detail than thicker inks. Transparent inks, however, will not appear bright on fabric. There are inks made especially for stamping on fabric, and Tulip® has fabric ink and stamp pads in a wide range of colors.

The stamp pad helps distribute the color evenly, giving the print its characteristic look. Use slight pressure to ink the stamp. Ink can be brushed on using either a bristle or foam brush. For larger, hand-made stamps, a beveled foam brush will work. Experiment to determine the right consistency and amount of ink. Felt-tip pens (such as Niji or Marvy® markers) can be used directly on the stamps for multicolored prints. Direct coloring works best on small stamps, as larger areas may dry out before the inking is completed.

Fabrics

Smooth, shiny fabrics (satin, chintz, polished cotton) give clearer impressions than coarser fabrics, with muslin being a good starter. For permanent prints your fabric must be free of surface treatments and must withstand the required heat setting. Any piece not requiring washing offers more flexibility in fabric choice. Fabrics which can't withstand heat setting should be ironed with a paper over the top at the maximum heat they can tolerate.

Stamps printed on white or light colors will have the most contrast and brilliance. Inks or thinned textile colors will, like dyes, allow background colors to show through. The addition of an opaquer (or the use of opaque acrylic paint) will be necessary to print over a light color. Opaquers dry fast, so add only the amount required for coverage. For washability, let prints cure for a day or two after heat setting. Heat set one color before adding another when shapes touch or overlap. Press on the reverse side of the fabric, or cover the design with paper.

Alignment

To center prints on blocks, first fold the fabric in half and crease it with a fingernail. Crease again in the opposite direction and diagonally, if needed. The folds serve as guides for centering, and for printing multiples.

To stamp images in circles, fold fabric in half and press lightly. Fold again at right angles, then continue forming wedge shapes in the cloth to serve as guides. Make several stamp prints on paper, cut out the paper images, and place them on the fabric to determine your arrangement. This is also helpful in determining placement for prints on garments.

Cut-out stamped paper prints are also helpful in placing multiple overlapping images. For example, if you want to stamp an entire chorus line of yourself, first print one image on paper and cut it out carefully on the lines. Then make your first print on fabric, and cover it with the paper cut-out before making the second print, which will overlap it. The second image now appears to be behind the first.

Another way to align your design is to cut a window the size of your stamp in a sheet of paper. When you have determined where the print is to go, place the window over that area and stamp within it.

CHAPTER 7

Adding Color

Even though stamp prints are essentially one-color prints, additional colors can easily be added. Use permanent markers or paint over the images with textile paint, as described in Hand Painting. Transfer dyes, crayon transfers, and dye sticks are all great for coloring stamped images. Embellishments with thread add texture as well as color, and French knots are especially effective.

Bonnie Peterson-Tucker
Break the Silence, 54" x 44"
photo: Bonnie Peterson-Tucker

In Bonnie's multi-hued village, each house lifts up to reveal hidden images and messages. Under the houses are collages of photo-transferred apartments, buildings, and realtors' listings, along with poignant rubber-stamped quotations regarding abuse.

making
YOUR OWN stamps

It's exciting to find and buy new stamps, but the satisfaction of making (or devising) your own stamps tops it all. For beginners, the eraser end of a pencil makes a perfect small stamp for polka dots or for stars, moons, squares, or half-circles. I've seen these little erasers carved into hexagons for miniature Grandmother's Flower Gardens and squares for Triple Irish Chains. For larger stamps, many designers particularly like the Staedtler Mars Plastic Grand erasers or Staedtler's carving block, which is about 3" x 4". Among other favorites are RubKleen®, Magic Rub, and Artgum® erasers. Adhesive-backed materials like Sure-Stamp™ simplify stamp-making. White vinyl or Pink Pearl® erasers carve well, and a very large size (for big mistakes, apparently) is also available. (This is considered a novelty item, so it is more likely to be found in an airport gift shop than at a stationers.)

Calligraphers may enjoy creating an alphabet from any of a variety of erasers which carve easily with an X-Acto knife and retain sharp edges. Letters can first be pencil-drawn on paper, then the paper can be placed face down on the eraser and burnished to transfer the pencil line to the eraser. This will reverse the letter so it prints correctly.

SOURCE LIST

Flexible printing plates, 1, 3, 22, 34

Stamp erasers, 1, 3, 4, 6, 7, 8, 22, 34

The potato carving you did in the third grade is still a valid way to make a stamp—especially if you like casual, loosely-printed designs. Carrots, potatoes, apples, and turnips work well, as they are inexpensive, firm, and have built-in handles. A clean, smoothly cut surface is essential for a good print. Use a sharp knife and don't saw with it. Vegetable stamps will last longer with refrigeration and a sealable plastic bag.

Kata Patton
One Can't be Angry When One Looks at a Penguin, 9" x 17"

Kata's penguins were cut from pink erasers to face both east and west. A separate stamp was cut for the bow ties, and letters were printed from her hand-carved alphabet. She inked letters with a foam brush or pressed her stamps onto a piece of felt which was coated with Hunt Speedball Textile Screen Printing Ink. As Kata likes to use hand pressure in printing her stamps, she prefers to have no handles.

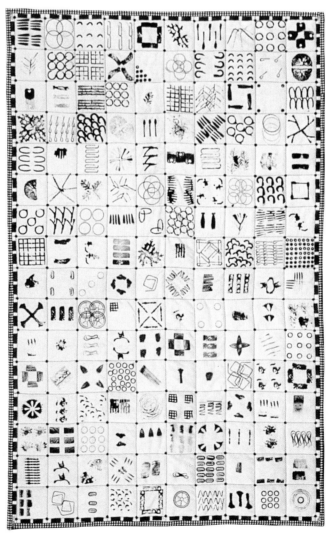

Jeanne Williamson
What's What, 49½" x 39½"
photo: David Caras

Stamping with just about anything at hand, Jeanne started collecting her "treasures" as she walked her son to school, and many of those objects found their way into her work. Working on a large piece of white brushed-denim, she first pencil-lined it into a 3" grid pattern. She then stamped with paper clips, Q-tips®, branches, spools, folded cardboard, berry baskets, an orange, and bow tie pasta (among other things) onto the cloth. She used a pencil eraser to stamp the grid intersections, knowing her pencil lines would wash out. She stitched the grid lines back in when she quilted and finished the panel.

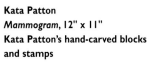

Kata Patton
Mammogram, 12" x 11"
Kata Patton's hand-carved blocks
and stamps

Kata's message in *Mammogram*
is printed with a combination of
five hand-carved blocks and
stamps. She used linoleum cutting
tools on Speedball Speedy Cut
Printing Blocks, carving linear
patterns into the background.
The alphabet was carved from
plastic erasers.

Jeanne Williamson
Garden in Front of the Lattice
45" x 43"
Detail of *Garden in Front of
the Lattice*
photo: David Caras

Jeanne printed with Deka Fabric
Paint on whole cloth with 1"-cube
Artgum erasers, some cut into
circles or triangles. She drew a grid
(in pencil) as a guide and
overlapped colors for transparent
effects. As a teacher, Jeanne
worked extensively with
vegetable prints. She found that
by cutting oranges, artichokes,
squash, and onions and placing
them face-down on paper
toweling a day before printing,
they lost enough liquid to
print easily.

Katy J. Widger
Purple Flower Woman, 55" x 55"
photo: Ken R. Wigder

Katy used only fabrics which she hand-painted or printed, giving her control over color, intensity, and density of prints, and making this quilt uniquely hers. Stamps and block prints of all kinds enrich and embellish her fabrics, and one of her favorites is the potato print. Carved potatoes hold dye and print well, give good detail, last for two days (if refrigerated overnight), and are disposable. Katy uses a variety of textile paints and dyes (including PROChem®'s Textile Ink and Setacolor® Opaque), but for her linoleum block prints she prefers oil-based inks.

Adhesive-Backed Stamps

Thin layers of stamp material with self-adhesive backings are sold as flexible printing plates, available under such names as Sure-Stamp, Pen Score Flexi-Cut®, and Poly Print®. They can be glued to wood, clear acrylic, or <u>foamboard</u> for easy handling. Fun Foam® is a thicker material, so the unwanted printing of background areas is less likely. A double layer of stamp material lifts the design to help make clean prints. Fun Foam is most suitable for simple shapes, as details cannot be easily carved. Any kind of foamboard can be used as the stamp material itself, so don't relegate it to being only the base.

Clays

Modeling clay, Super Sculpey III®, or Fimo® can be shaped into stamps and used as they are or baked for permanence. Roll Sculpey into a smooth, flat piece, and bake it at 275°F for 40 minutes. Level the baked stamp by sanding, then carve with linoleum-cutting tools.

Foam Pads, Sponges

Insoles, such as Dr. Scholl's® foot pads, make great stamps and can be easily cut. The insole holds paint nicely; but, if it dries out, it will be difficult to rinse later. A thin kitchen sponge or a finer-textured foam sponge is also inexpensive and easily cut. If you are working with children, pre-cut the foam sponge to fit a wood block. Then have the children cut designs with scissors from the thin foam before adhering the foam to blocks.

Inner Tubes

An inexpensive source of rubber-stamp material is an inner tube. You can get dozens of stamps from one old tube (Well, you can get just as many from a new inner tube, but most garages will give you an old one free.) Take a paper grocery bag with you to carry it home, hose it down thoroughly, and wash it with soapy water to prepare it for cutting. I usually cut up a tube immediately and throw away all unusable parts. Cut the rest into pieces (about 6" x 8") which are easy to handle and store. With scissors the rubber cuts like butter, so it's a cinch for children. Avoid areas of the tube which have raised seam lines, which will transfer, as well as those from the inside curve, which refuse to be flattened. Stamps from rubber will work best if they are glued to a wood base.

Miscellaneous Stamps

All kinds of household objects can be used for printing. Use the round ends of corks as they are, or carve into them. Anything that will hold some paint can be used. Flat rubber bowl scrapers or even jar rings can be used to stamp. Sink stoppers, potato mashers, and the rubber pads used in sinks will have patterns or textures that will transfer. Look around your own kitchen with a sharp eye for printing materials. Metal tools will also work, though they don't hold paint well.

Handles

Stamps are easier to use if there is a handle or a convenient way to grasp them. Most eraser stamps are thick enough to be picked up easily. The pencil eraser has a built-in handle which makes it fun to use. Put small stamps on spools or wood blocks. Adhere larger ones to foamboard, clear plastic boxes, or Plexiglas, which being transparent, makes it easy to align prints. Small wood scraps also work great and are often available from cabinetry shops.

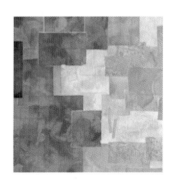

Improvised Stamp Pads

An advantage to making your own stamp pads is flexibility in size, which is important if you are also making your own stamps. Changing colors and paints is then a simple matter, and pads in which colors have become mixed or have dried out can be tossed away, since they are inexpensive.

To make a stamp pad, use any flat and non-porous surface (aluminum foil, a plastic plate) on which to lay a felt pad. First wet the felt and squeeze it nearly dry. Brush water-based <u>textile paint</u> onto the pad. Some stampers add a layer of muslin over the felt to avoid picking up lint. Two or three layers of heavy Pellon® fleece or other non-woven material makes a good pad and no muslin layer is necessary. Fun Foam has an excellent surface for a pad. Sponges offer a coarser texture but can be used. They tend to stiffen somewhat as they dry. Fashion Stamp Ink Pads (from Tulip Productions) are pre-cut pieces of a light foam-like material which work well. Cover all pads with plastic wrap or a sandwich bag when not in use.

Inks

Water-based textile paint makes stamping on fabric permanent. Brush textile paint onto a moist stamp pad, thinning as necessary. Textile airbrush inks offer intense but thinned colors and have a good consistency for stamping. Pour airbrush ink directly onto a pad. The right consistency is important—thin enough to print easily and heavy enough to show the color. Liquitex is somewhat more opaque than Deka or Versatex, though all work well. Eurotex makes an opaque white which can be mixed with their colors for printing lights on darks. Delta Fabric Paints® come in metallic colors and in handy squeeze bottles (great for inking pads).

Cleaning

All stamps will need to be cleaned occasionally, as paint tends to clog the open areas of the stamp. Clean stamps with sudsy water immediately after use. A soft-bristle toothbrush will remove paint from crevices. For other than water-based paints, follow the cleaning directions that accompany the inks.

Remove permanent inks from stamps with water that has a few drops of dishwashing detergent in it, scrubbing lightly if necessary. After stamping on fabric, immediately press the stamp down firmly on a scrap of paper or cloth to help remove excess paint or dye. To prevent their drying out during use, place stamps face down on a moistened pad. If you must leave your work, slip the stamps in a plastic bag and seal it shut.

Alphabet sets usually come in a box with slotted areas to keep the letters in order. It would be chaos to locate individual letters without storing them this way, though it is usually recommended that stamps not be stored face down on paper. I use a piece of <u>clear wrap</u> under the stamps to protect them.

TROUBLESHOOTING FOR STAMP PRINTING

Problem: Stamped fabric prints are incomplete or have flaws.
Solution: Make sure the printing surface is smooth.
             Use more pressure on the stamp.
             Touch up flaws with Niji markers or Pigma Micron® pens. Touch up black prints with any permanent marker, such as Pilot SC-UF® or Sanford's Sharpie.
Problem: Corners of the stamp blocks get inked and transfer to cloth.
Solution: Ink the stamp carefully, wipe corners clean before printing.
             Use a flat pad. A worn pad may let the corners of the stamp touch the pad.
             Cut or carve the corners of the stamp away.

Erika Carter
Journey, 46" x 66"
photo: Howard Carter

Erika begins her work by painting one- to six-yard lengths of cotton. She then uses sponge brushes to repaint and stamp additional pieces of silk organza. Natural sponges, a wallpaper paste brush, a wet round bristle brush, and a potato masher add a rich organic textural surface making each print unique. After tearing and stacking her fabrics, she arranges them and pins the shapes in place. She then machine stitches, applying everything in one process, working from the outside edges toward the center. The artist suggests a journey or a wandering path that goes in either direction, inviting, but not limiting, movement.

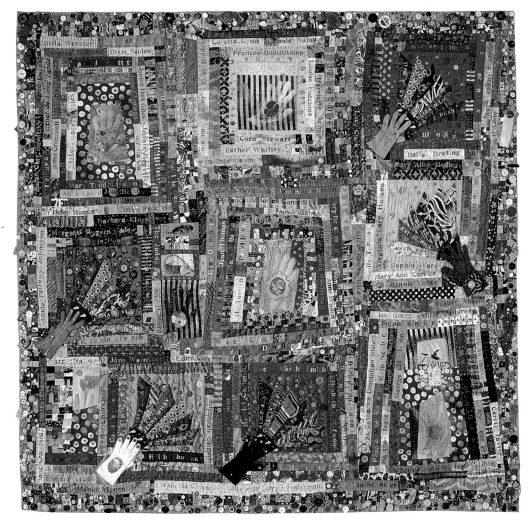

Jane Burch Cochran
Coming Home: Kentucky Women Quilt, 78" x 81"
photo: Carina Woolrich

Hundreds of names, including the famous and the not-so-famous, fill the colorful strips and ribbons of Jane's quilt. A list of the womens' names and accomplishments are tucked into an envelope sewn to the quilt back. Using a rubber stamp alphabet and Deka textile paint, Jane printed the text in confetti-like colors on printed and painted cloth. As she prints, the first stamp is left in place to be used as a guide for the next. Any imperfect letters are touched up with Prismacolor. The hands, which reach out across the blocks, are painted, printed, or are appliquéd gloves (with button nails). The entire colorful and exuberant piece is embellished with hundreds of buttons.

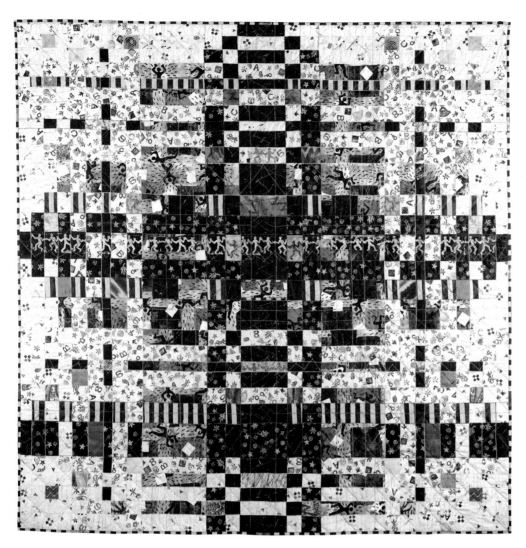

Natasha Kempers-Cullen
Jazz, 74" x 74"
photo: Dennis Griggs

To print the fabrics for *Jazz*, Natasha used a series of block prints carved from a flexible material called **E-Z Cut®**. She printed her hand-painted fabrics using water-based paints. Other areas of the piece were textured with sponge prints. This painted and printed panel was then torn and reassembled by weaving. Natasha further embellished and enriched the panel with appliqué, machine quilting, and glass beads.

Erika Carter
Traces, 46" x 52¹/₂"
photo: Howard Carter

Using an approach similar to that of *Journey*, Erika mixes her own paints of pure pigments and **PRO Chemical**'s low-crock medium into a watercolor consistency. This gives her the control she seeks over color intensities. In this panel Erika stamped some doll shoes, which she used on silk organza in a meandering pattern. The "traces," or steps, are a visual play, an allusion to time and history.

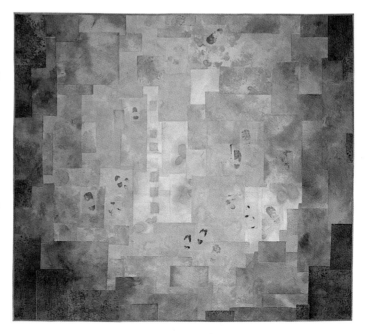

Midge Hoffmann
Intensive Gardening, 34" x 42"
photo: Steve Smith

Working with silk fabrics, Midge
garners kitchen gadgets (a wire
potato masher, a pastry cutter,
berry cartons, commercial
stencils from a crafts store,
needlepoint canvas), and pieces
she collects on her forays into the
second-hand store. These may be
used either as stencils or as
stamps. The berry carton, for
example, might be used as a
stencil over which her stiff-
bristled stencil brush is used, or
the bottom might be inked
and stamped. The artist uses
some iridescent silks over which
she prints with metallic, though
most of her printing makes use of
water-based textile paints and
acrylics. Her intensely colored
and richly textured fabrics are
fused on an Elna Heat Press and
machine stitched.

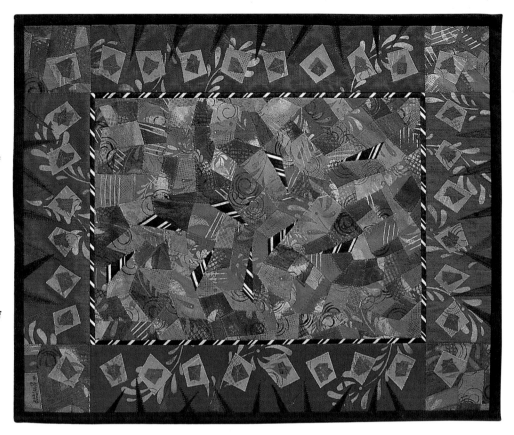

Therese May
Sampler #1, 28" x 44"
photo: Patrick Kirk

An old wet suit found its way into
Therese's studio, where she
incorporated it into the making
of this piece. She cut a stamp
from the rubbery (and easily cut)
material, then glued it to a wood
block with the fabric side up. The
nap of the wet suit held enough
acrylic paint to give a good, strong
print. She suggests that moleskin
will work as well and has the
advantage of a sticky back. After
printing the circle of cat heads,
Therese hand-painted the eyes
and noses. The horse head at
center was cut from mat board,
covered with metallic fabric,
painted, laminated to a larger
painted square, and sewn to the
panel. Other areas were hand-
painted, pieced, and embellished.

SOURCE LIST

Brayers, 1, 3, 19, 22, 34

Printing blocks, 1, 3, 7, 8, 22, 34

Katy Widger
Hand-carved linoleum blocks
photo: Ken R. Widger

A collection of Katy's hand-carved linoleum blocks is shown here. Each has been sawn off at the perimeter to avoid inked corners and to aid in alignment.

Some comonly available blocks include: Flexi-Cut, Flexible Printing Plate, Sticky Foam, Soft-Kut Print Blocks, Sax True Cut Printing Blocks®, E-Z Cut Blocks, and Speedball Speedy Cut.

Block prints, larger than stamps, require greater pressure to transfer the paint, and various presses are available. Hunt Speedball makes several small home presses. There are also etching presses, art presses, or litho presses which provide pressure without heat. Some printers hammer their blocks to apply pressure.

Wood blocks offer a method we are all familiar with—areas are cut or gouged from the wood, leaving raised areas to print. All block prints work similarly. Many new block materials are easily carved, and some thin blocks can be cut out and applied to a rigid backing.

Among the many methods used by Karen Felicity Berkenfeld in her *Three Rivers* panel, page 137, is a block print using Flexi-cut. To print the figures of three women at the top she first made a pencil drawing of the image. The drawing, placed face down on the Flexi-Cut, was burnished to transfer the image. This reversal, when printed, would look like the original. Placing the block on a hard, smooth surface, Karen started cutting it like a jigsaw puzzle, lifting out all shapes that would be printed in the same color. Paper was peeled off the back of the Flexi-Cut and the pieces were adhered to a clear Plexiglas or heavy Mylar plate. Karen determined which parts of this design would be most difficult to register and started there. The lines of the shawl, for example, would be printed first, and it would require care to fit the blue squares within that grid. The pieces for the blue squares were placed face down and sticky side up, and aligned over the red print. A piece of Plexiglas was laid over that and hand pressure made the small pieces stick to it. This prepared the second block. Subsequent colors were added the same way. Very small details, such as features, were hand painted.

Karen Felicity Berkenfeld
I Am Living a Quiet Life on the Upper Westside, 40" x 40"
photo: Karen Bell

This is Karen's tongue-in-cheek comment on the serenity of city living. In this vital and energetic piece she has combined linoleum block (for the skyline and the black and white patterns), Flexi-Cut (for the red and blue blocks with figures), commercial fabrics, and collographs. These various techniques join in a dynamic combination of color and design.

Karen Felicity Berkenfeld
Three Rivers, 53" x 48"
photo: Karen Bell

Karen prints with water-based paints, for which the standard rubber brayers are not suited. Instead she uses a foam brayer or a very small roller (one made for printing latex). As the nap disappears on the roller, it gets easier to use, and practice helps develop a feel for the amount of paint and pressure required. The center panel of this piece is made from a series of linoleum block prints. Two collographs are pieced to make up the panel at the bottom. A piece like this one requires a couple of dozen blocks to complete.

Kata Patton
Detail of *Save the Elephants*
Hand carved stamp

Kata used linoleum block cutting tools and a No. 11 X-Acto knife to carve her elephant stamp from Speedball Speedy Cut. At left, a detail of her panel shows the block print on commercial fabric. The linear pattern resulted from the way she carved the background area.

Karen Felicity Berkenfeld
Sweet Wings, 36" x 36"
photo: Karen Bell

In *Sweet Wings,* Karen combines collographs, linoleum blocks, and stamps. Her collographs are made up on cardboard or chipboard on which she carves or gouges out the linear designs. She then covers the remaining areas with shapes and textures—anything from leaves to coffee grounds, as long as the textures are low-relief. The shapes are adhered with gesso, and the finished piece is sealed in gesso and coated with Krylon. Paint is then applied to the collograph and printed in an etching press. In this panel the honeycomb blocks are cut from Flexi-Cut, the large honey bee is a linoleum block, the small bees are rubber-stamped, and other areas are collograph.

MONOPRINTS

Monoprints are, as the name suggests, single or one-of-a-kind prints. While it is a method developed for printmakers working on paper, it adapts well to fabric.

WHAT YOU NEED

Plate for paints (glass, Plexiglas, or any hard, smooth, non-porous surface)

Textile paints

Brushes, sponges, or brayers

PFP fabric

Newsprint

Iron and board

THE PROCESS

1. Using brushes, sponges, or brayers, spread paint on the plate to create the original. Avoid a heavy layer of ink, blotting with tissue or newsprint if necessary.
2. Cover original with fabric.
3. Press with hands or a brayer to transfer paint to fabric.
4. Dry and heat set.

Once the paint is brayered or brushed onto the glass, it can be textured in various ways. Scratched or scraped patterns will transfer, as will brush strokes or stippling. Experiment to find the methods most appropriate for your use. Sometimes a second or even a third print can be made from the inked plate, but the first will be strongest and brightest. No two will be identical.

Resists can be used on the fabric itself before monoprinting. Strips of masking tape will resist the monoprint to create lines or stripes. Any iron-on resist creates a negative area in the monoprint.

TROUBLESHOOTING FOR MONOPRINTS

Problem: Colors of the fabric print aren't like the original.

Solution: With two or more layers of paint, only the top layer may transfer.

A mirror-image reversal occurs with monoprinting, so prints will look different.

Problem: Some areas are solid paint with no patterns or lines showing.

Solution: Use less paint.

Use less pressure in printing.

Deborah Melton Anderson
Will there Ever Be Another Tick-Tack-Toe Chicken?, 33" x 36"
photo: Kevin Fitzsimons

Using water-based textile paints, Deborah made a series of monoprints to create the tick-tack-toe designs. Using brayers to spread the paint over a sheet of glass, she then drew, scratched, and further painted. These designs were transferred to cloth using hand pressure. The beaded chicken is an auction find. In the background, stitched circles of cloth and string were covered with dye transfer paper and heat set. When fabrics and strings were removed, the pattern remained. Lettering at the top of the panel is from a newspaper and has been embellished with colored pencils.

Linda Steider
Daydreams III . . . the Ride
36" x 24"
photo: Bill Bachhuber

Linda combines an array of techniques including monoprinting, hand painting, and various shibori methods. Transfer medium was used for the cars and monoprinting for the hearts and figures. All were fused in place. Monoprinted figures were created using a technique from Elizabeth A. Busch, involving the use of a cement spreader to create linear patterns in the monoprint. In Linda's adaptation she painted the fabric in several colors, then applied a second layer of paint over the first and scraped lines through it. The figure was then cut out of that fabric and fused to the background. Figures in the lower section were made in an unusual way. The artist folded the fabric into three sections, then drew the figure in stitches that served as a barrier when it was over-painted.

NATURAL FORMS

Take a handful of anything in nature and you have an extravagance of beautiful variations. Few printmakers can resist this inexhaustible resource, and inevitably, leaves, fish, ferns, spider webs, and evergreens find their way onto fabric. The same images have been used with copiers, printers, disperse dye, photo silk-screen, blueprinting, and discharge. This section will present the use of <u>natural forms</u> as printing plates.

leaf hammering

Leaf hammering is a method of transferring the delicate patterns of leaves to cloth. It is an ancient technique, of special interest to dyers. Linda Ligon wrote about it in *Handwoven Magazine*, June 1983. Iris Aycock seems to have single-handedly revived it and uses it to make her beautiful and unique quilts. She says leaf hammering is a method used by Cherokee women, who used wood ash as the fixer. One Cherokee woman who hammered leaves remembered her grandmother using this method, who in turn remembered her grandmother using it. After much experimenting with plants and dye procedures, Iris has developed her own method and shares it with us.

WHAT YOU NEED

Natural PFP fabric
Alum
Fresh leaves
Mechanic's hammer
Plastic wrap
Washing soda (or PROfix)
Synthrapol
Pad of newsprint
Masking tape
Drawing pens (optional)

THE PROCESS

1. Mordant the fabric, and dry it. (See instructions below.)
2. Place fresh leaves, vein sides down, on fabric, and use masking tape to secure them.
3. Turn the fabric over.
4. Cover with plastic wrap.
5. Place on a pad of newsprint.
6. Hammer over leaf until you see color coming through fabric.
7. Remove tape and leaves. Dry.
8. Dip in soda solution or paint with PROfix. (See instructions below.)
9. Cover with plastic wrap and leave 6-8 hours.
10. Wash fabric in Synthrapol.
11. Outline leaves in ink, if desired.

MORDANT:

The PFP fabric requires a mordant which makes the fibers more receptive to dye. Among the safest and simplest is this one. For one yard of fabric:

Dissolve:

2 tablespoons alum in

1 pint hot water. Cool.

Add:

1 teaspoon washing soda, dissolved in a little hot water.

When bubbling diminishes, add to 1 gallon water, at room temperature.

Add fabric and stir for 1 to 2 minutes, leave overnight, then hang to dry.

Pick your leaves after all your materials are assembled, since fresh leaves make better prints. Iris has successfully printed with Virginia creeper, sweet gum, wisteria, sumac, walnut, hickory, oak, tulip, poplar, kiwi, paulowinia, grape leaves, ferns, pine needles, and a few flowers. Since the dye in the leaves must not dry out, hammer immediately after picking. Use a sturdy, firm surface for hammering (like a butcher's block). A mechanic's hammer (or deadblow hammer) has rounded edges and avoids edge marks. As you hammer, liquid from the leaves will seep into the fabric. When you can see the leaf shape, remove the tape and leaf fragments and let the piece dry. The fabric must then be fixed.

FIXATIVE:

Soda Solution:

Dip the printed fabric in a solution of

1/2 teaspoon washing soda to

1/2 gallon water.

or paint the image with PROfix.

Cover the cloth with plastic wrap and leave 4 to 6 hours. Longer time gives a darker image.

Washing soda seems best for flowers and PROfix for tree leaves.

A final washing in hot water with Synthrapol completes the process. To make it easier to outline the leaves in ink, stabilize it by ironing freezer paper to the back of the dry fabric. A fine-line black permanent marker such as Pigma Micron can be used. Iris prefers to use a technical drawing pen (like Rapidograph®) which she fills with Deka silk dye instead of ink. The fabric must be heat set and is then ready to be used.

Hammered leaves vary in terms of permanence. When trying a new leaf, Iris hammers and completes a print, then pins it to the wall, where for six months it is exposed to bright light. If the print remains, she considers it permanent enough to use. Some will fade after a few months. The time of year (in the tree's growth cycle) affects dye permanence. Early spring leaves release more dye and brighter dye than late summer leaves.

This entire process is addictive, and lots of fun. Almost everyone who tries it enjoys it and finds the hammering a great way to work off aggressions or frustrations.

Iris Aycock
Philodendron and Kiwi
50" x 47¹/₂"
photo: Iris Aycock

Fine-line outlining of the leaves sharpens the image in Iris's leaf-hammered quilt. Leaves from the vines of cardinal flowers, which do not give a strong dye, offer a soft pattern.

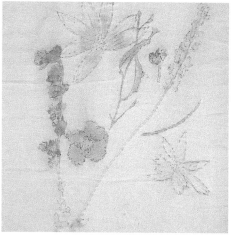

Erleen Leinsteiner
Detail of *Flowers*

These delicate pale colors were transferred with leaf hammering, then outlined using Micron® pens. Erleen's yellow and purple garden flowers turned to golds and browns.

Iris Aycock
Sassafras and Reel, 41" x 40¹/₂"
photo: Iris Aycock

Another technique has been incorporated by Iris in this panel. Shapes were cut from freezer paper and ironed onto the fabric; leaf hammering then transferred dye to the open or unprotected areas to create the reels.

leaf prints

Natural forms with flat surfaces make wonderful stamps—and leaves are the most obvious examples. The printing of fish is an ancient Japanese art still practiced today. In these processes the inked leaf or fish becomes the printing plate. There is an organization, The International Nature Printing Society, (see Bibliography page 173) devoted to printing botanical specimens, flowers, leaves, etc., and to sharing their information.

WHAT YOU NEED

Leaves

Textile paint or ink

Two brayers or beveled foam brushes

A smooth surface (glass, Plexiglas, cookie sheet) on which to spread paint

Scrap paper, or unprinted newsprint

PFP fabric

THE PROCESS

Wash leaves with detergent if they are dusty or oily. Particles may interfere with prints.

1. Drop a dollop of paint onto glass and brayer over it to get an even coat.
2. Place leaf, vein-side up, on newsprint.
3. Transfer paint to leaf with brayer or by brush.
4. Carefully pick up leaf, place it (painted side down) on fabric over a smooth surface.
5. Cover with newsprint, then use hand pressure or a clean brayer to transfer paint.

SOURCE LIST

Brayers, 1, 3, 19, 22, 34

Textile paints, 1, 3, 21, 22, 23, 34, 36

The requisite amount of ink and pressure will become obvious with practice. Larger shapes (a bough of cedar) will be harder to handle than single leaves. Several colors can be mixed on the glass, or you can create additional colors by printing one leaf that overlaps another of a different color. Adding extender to the paints will lighten the color without thinning the consistency.

Some designers prefer a foam roller or brayer, while others like plastic or rubber. In lieu of rollers use a sponge brush, or use a bristle brush for better control. Misting the fabric to be printed may help color absorption, but avoid using too much water. To create an overlay effect, print a leaf but leave it on the fabric. Overlap it with a second painted leaf and print. This creates an illusion of layers or depth.

Don't limit yourself to leaves! Remember that ferns and flowers work well, as do feathers, whole branches, mushroom spores, spider webs, shells, and shellfish. Fabric's flexibility also lends itself to use on three-dimensional forms.

CHAPTER 7

Betty Auchard
Detail of *Leaf Scarf*
photo: Richard W. Johns

Betty used clean, empty pump hair-spray bottles with Inko dyes, diluted four to five times. She arranged the leaves on her scarf and sprayed over and around them, to make negative prints. The leaves (now ink covered) were then picked up and used for printing, adding a positive print to develop a rich and complex overlay of patterns.

Betty Auchard
Untamed Garden, 44" x 61"
Detail of *Untamed Garden*
photo: Richard W. Johns

Betty hand stamped a wonderful array of leaves after cleaning them with a window-glass cleaner. She brush painted Inkodye onto her leaves, placed them (inked side down) on fabric, and let them rest a few seconds. This allowed the fabric time to absorb some of the dye. Light hand pressure was used to assure all-over dye transfer.

Ida Geary
Class Project, 28" x 54"
photo: Jonathan Perry

While teaching a botany and art class in the Golden Gate National Recreation Area, Ida had her students print the wallhanging shown here. Using Versatex paints, the students printed from leaves, seeds, mushrooms and fruits (halved), grasses, and even a plastic doll's foot found on the beach. Ida was instrumental in the founding of the International Nature Printing Society and writes extensively about leaf printing, both as a means of making botanical collections and as a form of art.

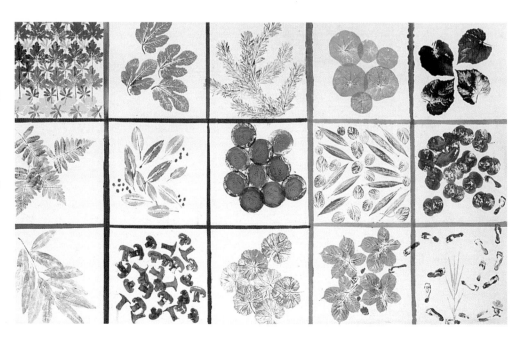

Betty Auchard
Four Patch Leaf Patterns, 32" x 54"
photo: Richard W. Johns

Betty printed leaves to record campsites on a cross-country trip. Before leaving home she cut and prepared fabric squares, allowing for extras. As both space and facilities in a motor home are limited, she had to eyeball the arragement on a tiny surface, but produced a wonderful series of blocks, each using four leaf prints.

Janet L. Paluch
Vest, back

After spreading a thin layer of Versatex on Plexiglas, Janet ran a brayer over it to pick up an even coat of paint. She then rolled the brayer over a fresh leaf. The inked leaf, face down on her cloth, was covered with paper, and rolled with a second clean brayer. Some of the prints are nearly opaque—others are transparent, showing the vein pattern. Janet quilted around the leaves in a dark brown.

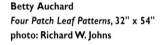

Vickie Schumacher
Morning Glories, 18" x 12"
photo: Vickie Schumacher

**Vickie printed from both flowers
and leaves with the stems adding
an important element to the
design. As they are difficult to
handle, she uses tweezers to carefully lift and place the stems.**

Vickie Schumacher
Poinsettias, 36" x 36"
photo: Vickie Schumacher

**Vickie's leaf prints on pieces
of linen needlework make
remarkable use of overlays, and
her color variations are exquisite.
Printed leaves, starting at the
center, were left in place as
protection when the next leaf was
placed on top of it. The nosegay
effect works perfectly within the
square of fabric.**

fish prints

Gyotaku is the ancient Japanese art of fish printing. Traditionally, the fish is cleaned and inked, then rice paper is placed over the fish and it is rubbed to transfer the ink. The prints were used to record the size and type of fish caught, and are both beautiful and detailed.

A variation of this process can be achieved using fabric. Having only read about it, I described it to a class in Anchorage who were eager to try it. One class member brought in two fish, and we experimented with remarkable results using Versatex on cotton muslin.

SOURCE LIST

Fish (you're on your own!)

Modeling clay, 1, 3, 22

PFP fabric, 38

Textile paints, 1, 3, 21, 22, 23, 34, 36

WHAT YOU NEED

Fish

Brushes, ¹/₂" to 1" wide (one for each color)

Textile paint

PFP fabric

Modeling clay (optional) or pins

THE PROCESS

1. Wash the fish and place on a flat surface. Press fins into modeling clay to keep them in position (or pin them).
2. Paint textile paint to cover fish.
3. Place fabric over fish, using light hand pressure.
4. Lift fabric. Dry and heat set.

The fish should be fresh, kept cold, and printed within 24 hours; otherwise, freeze the fish and thaw it for printing. Flounder, bass, perch, and rockfish work well. Fish with large or rough scales and spines give interesting prints.

Ann Bae Machado
Detail of *Quill Back*
photo: Ann Bae Machado

Ann cleans her fish with table salt or detergent to remove the slick protective coating. She then covers the fish with silk and adds her paint, mixing it as she applies it. Only the eyes are added by brush. Her very fine, light-weight silk is mounted over canvas and she then paints the background.

Vickie Schumacher
Detail of *Walleye*, T-shirt
photo: Vickie Schumacher

Vickie used Deka paints to make her fish print on a T-shirt. Using two colors of paint which she carefully blended for the body of the fish, she hand painted the background.

There is a protective mucous-like coating over fish that must be removed for clear prints. Wash the fish thoroughly with soap and water. The fish may be gutted (then stuffed with paper towels) or left ungutted. In either case, the anus should be plugged with paper to avoid any leaks on your print. In class, we cleaned the fish with acetone, which tended to dry the surface and help the paint adhere. We did not gut or plug it.

Apply paint to the fish with a brush, foam brush, or brayer, painting head to tail. Then brush in the opposite direction to force paint under the scales. If the surface tends to dry, mist with water. Place fabric over the fish and gently press to transfer the paint. Some printers prefer to mist the fabric lightly before placing it over the fish. Be sure the paper beneath the fish is clean, as any paint there may transfer.

There are two basic approaches to fish printing—direct and indirect printing. In direct printing, the fish is painted and the fabric or paper is placed on top to transfer the ink. The indirect method, preferred by Ann Machado, involves placing silk on the fish and then applying the paint. She uses a cotton ball wrapped in silk to dab the oil-based paint onto her silk. Traditionally, the fish was covered with a rice paper (or similarly absorbent soft paper) and misted with a spray of water. When dry, paint was applied to the paper. Most fish printers hand painted the eyes in afterwards. Silk picks up every detail and tends to wrap easily over the rounded fish. Muslin is easy to handle and absorbs the dye well. Try a variety of fabrics, including dyed or painted backgrounds. Once the fish prints are dry and heat set (if appropriate), additional color may be added with colored pencils or by hand painting.

RAISED OR METALLIC SURFACES

Images on cloth can be given dazzling three-dimensional or metallic surface treatments with these methods. Both involve the use of a second material, or carrier, to bind them to cloth.

embossing

SOURCE LIST

Embossing powders, 3, 8

Embossing involves the use of a powder which adheres to moisture. It is designed for use on paper but will work on cloth to some degree. When heated, the powder expands and adheres. Complete instructions come with the powders, available at craft and hobby shops.

A design stamped on cloth, or fabric run through a printer or copier, has enough moisture to hold the powder. Because cloth is more absorbent and less smooth than paper, toner does not stay on the surface in as even a layer; therefore, the embossing will not be as even. If you are using a printer, adjust it for a dense print. Use a copier on as dark a setting as possible without having the over-all go dark.

Stamping or screen printing offers better results because it is possible to ink more heavily. The heavier ink will hold the embossing powder and offer more texture. Smooth fabrics will give better results than textured ones.

foil

SOURCE LIST

Foiling Glue, 3, 8, 28, 34

Foils, 3, 8, 28, 34

Foils add wonderful metallic effects, though the reflective surface is difficult to photograph. Foils (such as Jones Tones) come in brilliant colors with a silver or gray backing. The foils will adhere to toner or glue. Aleene makes a glue especially for foils and others are generally sold with the papers.

Glue can be used to draw or paint, and when it is dry (up to 24 hours) the foil is placed (shiny or colored side up) on the glue area. It is then covered with a paper and ironed with a medium hot iron—though with some foils (such as Jones Tones), burnishing makes the transfer. As the foil sheet is removed, the metallic surface remains behind, enhancing the original with a bright reflective surface. Because of the texture of cloth, it will never be as smooth as when used on paper. By printing glue through a silk screen or Thermo-Fax screen, I've been able to foil lettering, photos, and detailed images.

If you run a fabric through the black and white laser printer, you should be able to foil it by burnishing, ironing or by running the fabric through the printer a second time. On the second trip, run it through blank (no printing) with the foil in place on top. Some printers will transfer the foil—but it must be the foil transferred by heat, rather than by burnishing.

Once a paper is lifted off the glue or toner, it may be evident that portions are untransferred. Use a new piece of foil and burnish again. Use the toe of the iron or burnisher to force the foil to stick. Any untransferred areas of foil can be reused, and repeats or overlays will not affect the print as glue will accept only one layer of foil. Always cover with paper before ironing.

Any method by which you can transfer glue to cloth will work for foiling: stamps, stencils, silk screens, or wood blocks. The glue must be washed off your screen or block before it dries.

Ritva

After screen printing the photo image on cloth using glue, I let it dry for a day then applied the foil the next day. The reflective surface is not captured in photographs but the cloth has metallic luster that is effective.

discharge printing

If you have ever splattered a bit of laundry bleach on one of your bright colored shirts, you are familiar with discharge dyeing. Nothing shows at first, and you're convinced the drops must have splashed elsewhere. An hour later you notice a clear white patch on your shirt. That's discharge.

Discharge chemically removes color from a pre-dyed piece of cloth. There are various ways of preparing and applying the bleaching agent to cloth—it may be thin or thick, liquid, gel, or powder, sprayed or painted. It may discharge on exposure to air, heat, or steam.

A bonus effect with discharge is that many dyes do not go directly to white—they may progress through other colors on their way. Discharge a black fabric, for example, and you may get a green, a beige or a gray. This chapter includes:

general information

liquid bleach discharge

thickened bleach discharge

other discharge agents

Discharge ranges from a relatively simple process (bleach in—color out) to a far more complex one. Home-studio methods using bleach incorporate lots of unanticipated variations, which is part of the fun. The processes described here involve the use of household chlorine bleach. Other discharge agents have their own guidelines.

WARNING: Read labels on discharge or bleach containers. Avoid eye or skin contact. Work outdoors or with adequate ventilation, and wear neoprene gloves and a mist respirator (from paint stores) if you are sensitive to bleach.

Fabrics

Cotton and rayon, both cellulose plant fibers, will discharge best with bleach, while wool and silk (animal or protein fiber) will be damaged by it. Avoid synthetics, which do not discharge well. While all natural fabrics are recommended, several designers have found that a 50/50 cotton/poly gives them satisfactory results. Do test pieces of any fabrics you intend for a major project. Heavy, more absorbent fabrics are less likely to run. Try mesh, corduroy, velveteen, and jacquard weaves for various effects.

I use a pre-tested cotton or rayon for classes, one I know will discharge dramatically. Always test cottons—some will bleach out while others will not budge. I sometimes buy small amounts ($^1/_4$ yard) of four or five different brands, then experiment with them. If a particular fabric in one line discharges, usually all other colors in that line will bleach out as well. Removing color from a dark value will create the strongest contrast. A discharge on yellow or pink will range from subtle to barely discernible.

To test fabrics, designer Lois Erickson takes a small plastic bag filled with a few tablespoons of bleach when she shops. She pops samples into the bag and soon knows if they'll discharge. Fiber artist Jane Dunnewold suggests taking a small vial of bleach to be used the same way. (Take your samples outside the fabric shop before testing!)

Prewash all fabrics to be discharged using:
$^1/_4$ teaspoon Synthrapol per 1 yard of fabric

This is important, since some <u>fabric finishes</u> interfere with the discharge. Others may contain chemicals which can mix with chlorine, which would create noxious fumes. To determine the fiber content of a swatch, make a simple match test—natural fibers burn, form an ash, and smell like singed hair—man-made fibers will melt and bead. Use caution.

Discharge Agent

The most convenient discharge agent to use is household chlorine bleach (sodium hypochlorite). It is inexpensive, readily available, and if handled carefully, relatively safe. The way it can transform fabric is indeed magical.

Other discharge agents include Rit Color Remover® (safe for silk), Formosul (for both cellulose or protein fibers), Jacquard's® Color Remover, and Rongalet-ST®. The specific discharge used, coupled with the particular fabric, determines the final color.

Stop-Agent

As bleach lightens color it also weakens fibers. Therefore, it is important to arrest the bleaching as soon as the desired color is achieved. Discharge is removed by thorough rinsing, or neutralized with a stop-agent. Some designers prefer to simply rinse the fabric and run it through a full wash cycle. Most use a mix of white vinegar and water, or hydrogen peroxide and water as a stop-agent while some prefer Anti-Chlor. In classes with limited access to water, we rinse for several minutes in a stop-agent. Then fabrics are taken home to be thoroughly washed. If washing is not thorough, the bleaching action may continue.

Stop-agents vary depending on the specific discharge used. For discharge with household bleach, use the recipe below.

Discharge can be used in almost any way that paint can be used. The viscosity of the discharge determines how it is applied. A fine line of bleach can be used for lettering, but it may bleed. A thicker mixture can be block printed or screen printed. Try various mixes, but start with plain household chlorine bleach.

WHAT YOU NEED	THE PROCESS
Household chlorine bleach (which contains sodium hypochlorite—commonly referred to as chlorine bleach)	1. Place fabric over a plastic drop cloth or a fiberglass screen in a well-ventilated area.
Stop-Agent	2. Apply bleach; allow color to discharge.
A plastic bucket containing:	3. Rinse thoroughly in stop-agent (3 to 5 minutes).
1 cup white vinegar and 1 gallon water or	4. Rinse in clear water.
1/2 cup hydrogen peroxide and 1 quart water	5. Run through a complete wash cycle.
Neoprene gloves	
Mist respirator	
Drop cloth (to protect work area)	
Rayon or cotton fabric (pre-tested)	

SOURCE LIST

Anti-Chlor, 31

Color Remover (Jacquard), 33

Formusol, 31

Mist respirator, 5, 21, 22

Needle tip applicator, 1, 3, 16, 22

Neoprene gloves, 5, 19

Rit Color Remover, 3, 4, 5

Rongalet-ST, 33

Spray bottle, 1, 3, 5, 22, 31, 33, 34

Synthrapol, 21, 31

LIQUID BLEACH DISCHARGE

Anyone who has used a jug of bleach knows this method. Experiment on small pieces of fabric—a four-yard length is much more difficult to manage.

Spraying Fabric

Bleach, straight from the jug, or mixed up to 50/50 with water, can be poured into a plastic spray bottle for direct use on fabrics. Spraying can be used to create shadings and soft lines.

A freezer-paper stencil, ironed onto the fabric, will limit the spreading of spray. It must be firmly applied (with a good hot iron). Stickers, masking tape, and self-adhesive shelf paper will all work, though the cloth should not be moved, as the spray has a tendency to lift the paper stencil from the cloth. Other objects such as grids, leaves, rice, blocks, plastic tools—anything that won't be hurt by bleach—will work as stencils. Lois Ericson likes mesh bags, lacey textures, shaped-foam cut-outs from packaging.

Martie Carroll
T-Shirt

Martie tore a figure from newspaper and placed it along with a fir bough to create a resist over the fabric. Using a spray bottle full of diluted bleach she sprayed over the resist. Once the bleaching started, Martie kept a close eye on the colors, and as soon as she saw the desired effect, she dipped the shirt in a water rinse, then in a vinegar/water stop-agent. After several rinses, she put the T-shirt through the wash cycle.

Susan Macy
Long-sleeved shirt

Susan discharged over branches of evergreen on a long-sleeved black shirt. A very fat little gecko, which she free-hand cut from heavy paper, served as a stencil. She then sprayed the shirt (outdoors) with a laundry spray bottle filled with 1/2 water and 1/2 bleach.

Drawing and Painting

Bleach can be brush painted directly onto cloth. As it is watery, the bleach will tend to run, especially on smooth, woven fabrics. Textured fabrics will absorb the liquid more readily. Pour a little bleach into a plastic or glass dish (one that won't tip) and use an inexpensive bristle or sponge brush to paint. If parts of the fabric are first painted with plain water, the bleach will make a soft transition into the wet areas. Remember that the bleach may ruin your brushes.

Small squeeze bottles filled with bleach can be used like pens for drawing. Draw the tip quickly over the fabric to prevent running.

Donalene H. Rasmussen
Ginkgo, 42" x 78"
photo: Donalene H. Rasmussen

Using a small plastic bleach-filled bottle with a screw-on metal tip, Donalene was able to draw fine lines on fabric. In *Ginkgo* the large leaves were pieced, but before they were appliquéd to the backing, she discharged the pattern. The fish were rubber-stamped, using a brayer to apply Versatex to the stamp. Small ginkgo leaves were stamped in a random pattern over the background.

Crumpled Fabric

Just crumpling or wadding up fabric before discharging creates intriguing textures. Wiping off the plastic drop cloth has yielded some spectacular results. This reminds us that for all-over patterns, just about any method which scatters the discharge will be effective. Areas of wet and dry fabric also alter the discharge pattern.

Manipulating Fabric

By folding, pleating, or gathering fabric before discharging it, you create protected areas to contrast with exposed ones. Brush or spray the discharge over the folds and gathers. Tying the fabric with strings will produce finer details and all-over patterns. Machine basting stitches can be used to manipulate the fabric, and can be easily removed after the masking process.

Lois Ericson
Vest

Lois discharges corduroy, jacquard weaves, and natural fibers of all weights. Her vest was discharged by wrapping and tying her fabric around a PVC pipe, then brushing bleach over the top. She uses a wide range of resists and stencils, from mesh bags to cardboard, over which she mists a thin spray of bleach.

CHAPTER 8

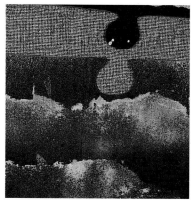

Torn cardboard resist

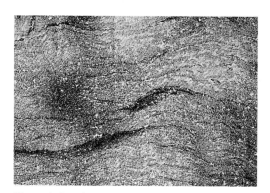

Cheesecloth resist

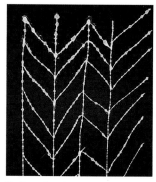

Syringe drawing resist

Examples of Lois's fabrics include torn cardboard, a syringe drawing, and an accordian-pleated fabric to which wood blocks were clamped before discharging. In the two other examples casement fabric was used over her material, creating distinct as well as soft patterns, and cheesecloth made undulating patterns.

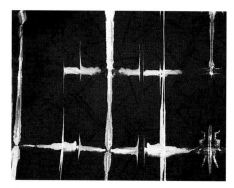

Clamped wood blocks resist

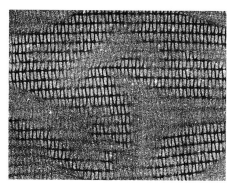

Casement cloth resist

Velda E. Newman
Geraniums, 82" x 98"
photo: Brent Kane

In her large appliqué panel, Velda used discharge in a painterly way to suggest leaf veining. After cutting out the leaves and arranging them, she used straight bleach and a dry-brush technique to create the areas of pale yellow-green. The fine lines were added with the use of a small squirt bottle (end cut off) filled with bleach and used as a drawing tool.

CHAPTER 8

Printing and Over-Painting

Straight from the jug, bleach can be used for sponge printing, block printing, or stamping. Pour a small amount of bleach into a stable, glass container, closing the jug until more is needed. Don't worry about drips—they just add pattern. A thickened bleach or discharge paste will offer more control.

Anytime a fabric does not turn out to your satisfaction, consider your discharge just a first step. Remove more color in subsequent discharges, or use the fabric as background over which to screen print, block print, hand paint, or over-dye. Or simply cut the material into strips or blocks and reassemble.

THICKENED BLEACH DISCHARGE

Observe all precautions. Use with good ventilation!

Adding a thickener to bleach gives it a consistency that is paint-like and more easily controlled for printing or painting. Add bleach to commercially available thickeners or mix your own discharge paste.

Dharma Trading Company has a Discharge Paste Color Remover which can be used on silk, cotton, or rayon. After it is applied and dried, the fabric is heat set with an iron, causing the discharge to activate and remove color. It has a strong ammonia smell and is neutralized by washing in Synthrapol. Jacquard's Discharge Paste can be applied, dried, and ironed with steam to develop the discharge.

In mixing your own paste, you can adjust the viscosity—as long as the mixture is not over half bleach. Mix only what you are going to use. Once bleach is mixed with the thickening agent, it will begin to dissipate, so use it immediately. Discard any leftover mixture.

An alginate/bleach mixture tends to get thinner as you use it. Monagum stays thicker longer. The thickener can be kept in the refrigerator for several months, but once bleach is added it begins to thin and weaken.

WHAT YOU NEED
Household chlorine bleach
Monagum (or other thickener)
Stop-agent
Neoprene gloves
Pre-tested fabric
Drop cloth or fiberglass screen

THE PROCESS

1. Place fabric on drop cloth or fiberglass screen.
2. Mix discharge paste. Chill bleach before adding it to the thickener.
3. Apply discharge paste to fabric.
4. When discharged, rinse in stop-agent.
5. Run through wash cycle with Synthrapol.

SOURCE LIST

Anti-Chlor, 31

Color remover, 21, 33

Discharge paste, 3, 21, 33

Pro-Monagum or PROthick F, 31

Sodium Alginate, 3, 21, 33

Thickener, 41

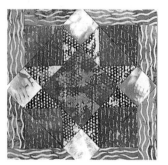

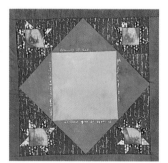

Elia Woods
Even Darkness Has Its Wonders
15" x 15" each
photo: Jenny Woodruff

Elia's four small panels show discharge in a variety of ways. Using Dharma discharge paste in a bottle with a metal tip point, she wrote stanzas of songs over portions of the background fabric. Other lettering was done with rubber stamps. Quotes from her own writing outline some of the squares, and solvent-transferred fusible appliqué, over-dying, and commercial fabric complete the work.

Since there are several thickeners on the market to which household chlorine bleach can be added, read the directions which come with the thickener. Generally, you will add:

Thickener:

3 tablespoons monagum thickener to

1 cup warm water

Stir or blend vigorously. Let it rest overnight (or several hours).

Stir again. Use at room temperature.

Some techniques require a thicker paste than others.

Thicker Bleach:

Measure: $\frac{1}{2}$ cup of the mixed thickener

Add: 1 tablespoon of chilled bleach at a time, up to $\frac{1}{2}$ cup

The more bleach you add, the thinner the solution gets and the faster it will discharge.

With less bleach, the thicker solution will discharge more slowly.

To stop the discharge, do any one of the following:

Option 1.

Rinse thoroughly in cold water, changing water several times.

Then run fabric through a full wash cycle.

Option 2. Immerse fabric in a stop-agent:

| 1 cup vinegar to | **or** | $\frac{1}{2}$ cup hydrogen peroxide to |
| 1 gallon water | | 1 quart water |

Option 3.

Run through a full wash cycle with Synthrapol.

Option 4. Rinse in Anti-Chlor solution:

1 teaspoon Anti-Chlor in

$2\frac{1}{2}$ gallons warm water

Then wash in hot water with Synthrapol.

Discharge paste can be used with a Thermo-Fax screen or silk screen for multiple prints. (Be sure the screen is polyester, as bleach will destroy silk.) Use the squeegee with pressure on the first pass, then less pressure on the second. That will allow for a thicker build-up of discharge on the fabric. A photo emulsion image will eventually dissolve from the bleach, but you can get many prints before that happens. A <u>contact paper</u> or <u>freezer-paper</u> stencil will work. <u>Thermal screens</u> will withstand repeated printings.

Stamps will pick up and hold a thickened discharge paste more readily than they will pure bleach. However, there is an irregular effect with the more liquid stamping that some designers find especially appealing. For block prints or large stamps, paint the discharge on with a foam brush. Or spread the paste onto a smooth surface and press the stamp onto it.

Ann M. Adams
Natural Soul, 45" x 45"
photo: Carina Woolrich

In this discharge piece, Ann first cut the nine squares of black cotton velveteen for the center of the quilt and discharged them by stamping. She devised an absorbent stamp which consisted of three layers cemented together—wood, then balsa, then felt cut into her stamp shape. She used a scroll saw to cut the wood block to the shape of the felt. This felt surface absorbed some of the discharge liquid, and was left to rest on the fabric for about 30 seconds. Ann mixed just one part household chlorine bleach to five parts thickener to make a mixture which stayed thick longer. When the discharge was finished, she stopped the bleaching with Anti-Chlor concentrate, then used a thick paint to add color. A reflective gold Lumière was used for the dots and linear patterns over the block.

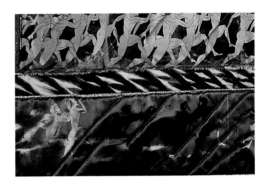

Barbara Sweeney
Violence Against Women, 45" x 36"
photo: Carina Woolrich

In Barbara's panel the stark faces and figures were discharge dyed by printing the discharge paste through a photo silk-screen onto black fabrics. Barbara used discharge with an alginate thickener. In the center area, white fabric was screen printed in red and black, then hand painted and dyed.

Jo Ann Giordano
Detail of *Men Who Run*
photo: Jo Ann Giordano

Jo Ann's piece shows images of figures that have been discharge printed. In the upper band the black fabric was discharged to a light brown using screen printing. The full quilt is shown on page 95.

OTHER DISCHARGE AGENTS

Any household products containing bleach are potentially good for discharge. Here are two of my favorites; they require no mixing and no handling of bleach. They are slower to discharge (sometimes taking overnight), but this less concentrated bleach applied for a longer period of time yields a similar result.

Dishwashing Gel

In situations where I don't want to pour and mix liquid bleach, I substitute Comet Gel®, which contains chlorine in a thickened base. Use any household dishwashing gel containing bleach. The gel has to be left on the fabric for a long time, since it is not a concentrated mixture. Sunlight aids in the discharge. A viscosity thickener (available from Welsh) can be mixed with dishwashing gel to give it a consistency better for screen printing.

The first time I screened with dishwashing gel containing bleach I assumed it had not worked, since it was very slow acting. I ignored the fabric, not even bothering to rinse it. By the next morning it was perfectly discharged. The advantage to using this gel over paste is its convenience and safety. I would let children work (supervised) with the gel, but not with the bleach.

Kris Vermeer
Rock Legend, 30" x 30"

Kris's drawings were first imaged onto a Thermo-Fax screen. She then used Comet gel as the bleaching agent, squeegeeing it through the screen and onto her fabric. It required several hours for the bleach to be effective. The lines next to the blocks were screen printed, with hand painted dots.

Cleanser Powders

Another ready-made bleach mixture is found in any household cleanser that has "bleaching action." Don't breathe the powder as you shake it out of the can. Since the bleach is dry, and requires water to activate it, the fabric can be moistened with a water spray before the cleanser is added. I've used <u>freezer-paper</u> <u>stencils</u> (ironed firmly onto fabric), then spritzed the fabric with water, blotted excess moisture off the paper stencil, and finally sprinkled on the cleanser. Areas can be shaded or speckled with gradations of discharge.

SOURCE LIST

Household cleanser containing bleach

Judith Content
Sumi, 59" x 49"
photo: Judith Content

Judith uses variations of discharge and shibori to produce stunning silk panels and kimonos. In *Sumi* she started with pieces of black Thai silk about 4 feet long by 10" or 11" wide. She stretched these on the diagonal, creating reed-like folds resembling grasses or narrow leaves. The silk in small bundles was wrapped around an empty wine bottle and secured with fine threads. Folded and tied areas resist alteration, retaining the original color. She discharged with lemon-scented Rit Color Remover, and sometimes dipped the silk in discharge, creating color gradations. When the desired amount of discharge was achieved, she arrested the action by dipping the fabric in cold water. Judith also works with white silk, which she ties similarly, using dyes instead of discharge. Her fabrics are torn into strips for reassembly. She then appliqués and quilts extensively.

Heart

A torn newspaper stencil was placed on the fabric and a spray of clear water dampened both paper and fabric. I then shook the powdered cleanser over the surface and left it overnight for the discharge to be effective.

CHAPTER 9

Polaroid transfers

The old superstition that a photo captures a part of its subject's spirit or soul seems perfectly reasonable to me. I find it impossible to discard or burn an old photo, and particularly if faces appear— even those I've never laid eyes on before. Some faces appeal to me (successfully) for rescue from their anonymity in antique shops. This association of the magical with photos adds another dimension to their use and seems particularly true with this transfer process. There is an immediacy with Polaroid that combines with the "other world" look of the transfers…a tentative, incomplete and antique look. This aspect of mystery, or of images that are only partially revealed, gives this transfer method a look that is totally unique. This chapter includes:

Polaroid transfer

emulsion transfer

POLAROID TRANSFERS

Polaroid transfer offers a unique combination of fabric painting with photo images. While it was developed primarily for transfer onto paper, it was almost immediately adapted to fabric. First attempts are often imperfect, and can be the most interesting, imparting a fresco-like appearance. The soft, subtle variations can be enhanced with pencils, dyes, or paints—often creating the look of watercolors. Polaroid transfer is sometimes described as a "cross-over art" —that is, one which balances on a fine line between photography and painting.

The process basically involves peeling apart an exposed Polaroid film, discarding the <u>positive</u>, and transferring the <u>negative</u> image to a receptor surface. While several methods of transfer are in use, this one is most commonly used and is the most versatile for non-photographers.

Polaroid transfer

The Polaroid process is trickier on fabric than it is on paper. Should you wish to practice on paper first, the process is similar. Polaroid has excellent publications available, has service centers in many states, and has a phone number for technical questions (800) 225-1618.

Patrice Jensen
Detail of Jacket

Transferred to cotton fabric and set into a jacket panel, Patrice's Polaroid transfers are like a walking photo album. The distortion at the edges adds the fragile look of another era.

WHAT YOU NEED
35 mm slide
Vivitar Instant Slide Printer (reproduces the slide image on Polaroid film)
Polaroid film (type 669 or 108)
Scissors
Squeegee or brayer
Hair dryer
X-Acto knife
Timer (or watch with a second hand)
Distilled water
<u>PFP Fabric</u>, natural fiber, at least 8" square
Masking tape

SOURCE LIST

Polaroid film, (photo shop)

Vivitar®, (photo shop)

THE PROCESS

1. Tape edges of fabric to a smooth counter or table top.
2. Spray with distilled water until wet (not soggy).
3. Roll with brayer to assure smooth contact.
4. Select a slide with intense, warm colors, and high contrast.
5. Load film into Vivitar.
6. Turn Vivitar Printer on. Place slide on viewing screen and position it. Move slide into the horizontal slot above viewing screen.
7. Set exposure one stop above normal.
8. Press exposure button. (Vivitar will enlarge 35 mm slide to fill Polaroid film as it exposes.)
9. Turn off the slide printer (to save batteries).
10. Pull exposed film from the Vivitar, first pulling the extended white tab to reveal the black tab. Grasp the black tab firmly and pull with a single smooth motion.
11. Immediately cut off the chemistry end of the film sandwich (the end opposite the pull tab, being careful to hold the image by the edges).
12. Allow 10-30 seconds processing time (from removal of film to when you peel the sandwich apart, separating the layers).
13. Set aside the positive (the shiny print you would normally keep), and apply the negative half, face down, on fabric. Once it makes contact, do not try to reposition. It will smear.
14. Cover with paper towel.
15. Use brayer, and roll for 10 to 15 seconds, with firm, moderate pressure.
16. Dry with a hair dryer for 90 to 120 seconds. Keep dryer 6" from negative and keep it moving.
17. Peel negative away very slowly, pulling on the diagonal. If the corner sticks, start at another corner. Use an X-Acto knife to cut through the chemical emulsion, if necessary.
18. Air dry. The transferred image may be pressed on the back of the fabric with a warm iron.

CAUTION: Avoid contact with gel, as these chemicals contain a caustic paste. Wear neoprene gloves, and avoid contact with eyes. If chemicals get on your hands, wash in water and then in a vinegar rinse. DO NOT allow children or food in the work area.

After exposure, Polaroid pictures usually develop in one minute. During that time the dyes migrate from the negative to the positive, creating the print image. Ordinarily, after the one minute of developing, you separate the film and toss the negative in the trash.

In image transfer, you wait just 10-30 seconds (or longer) before peeling the two layers apart. The negative is still active—colors are still moving or migrating. When the negative is placed face down on the fabric, the transfer occurs. It finishes processing, and then the negative is removed. Set the positive aside for emulsion transfer, page 165, or for use on paper.

A pan or bowl of water to which a cup of white vinegar has been added should be kept on hand. If you get chemicals on your hands, rinse them off, then neutralize them in the vinegar water. Wash and rinse thoroughly.

Peeling

Peeling, or separating the layers, arrests the dye movement. The time needed varies, but start with 10 seconds. Some new literature recommends 30 seconds. Since the cyan is the first color to transfer, prints may have a cyan bias. Reds and yellows take longer to develop. Therefore, a red, yellow, or amber filter (used in the Vivitar) will help balance color.

Cutting

When cutting off the chemical end of the film, keep the trim line narrow so as much edge as possible is retained. That will provide a color-change frame all around.

Vivitar

The Vivitar Instant Slide Printer is the most expensive aspect of this process—though if you get addicted, film costs will mount. The advantage of using a Vivitar is the possibility of duplicating images and the wide range of source material. Another method lets you bypass the Vivitar, working directly from a Polaroid exposure, but the Vivitar allows you to do your camera work where you have the transfer materials. A third method, projection printing, requires the availability of an enlarger and a darkroom.

Fabric

Natural fibers work best, and a fine silk gives the clearest prints. Polyester and acrylic seem to repel the film. Light colored fabrics are needed to retain light areas in a print. A slide of light and bright colors will transfer more easily than darks, which may become gummy.

Care

Polaroid transfer fabrics can be submerged in water for a light washing. Use no abrasive action. Press carefully on the wrong side with a warm iron.

Embellishing

Some artists like to scratch or draw on the Polaroid film before separating the layers. A scratch will force the gel out of the way, leaving a white line. Touch-up can be applied to the fabric with textile dyes or paints, Prismacolor pencils, or permanent markers.

Carolyn Skei
Apron

A Polaroid shot of a bunch of carrots provides an appropriate image for the apron shown here. Carolyn works primarily on paper, but this transfer was to cotton. It is pieced and stitched then padded and quilted.

Patrice Jensen
Polaroid Panel, 16" x 13"

Patrice's Polaroid transfers on cotton fabric are pieced into a wall panel. The irregular edges, which result from incomplete transfers, are characteristic of the method, adding an antique quality.

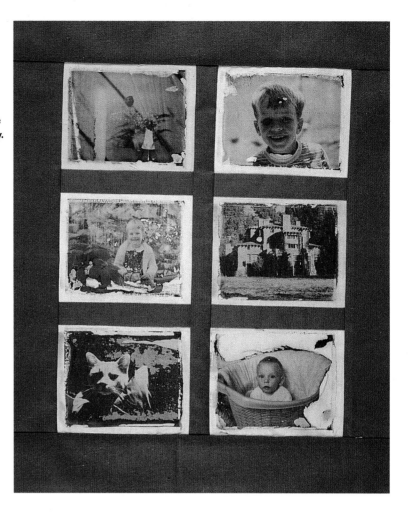

Patricia Malarcher,
Matrix 3, 11" x 8¹/₂"
photo: D. James Dee

A Polaroid collage was used to create the photo image in the center panel of *Matrix 3*. Patricia placed one Polaroid transfer over another, bonding them with matte medium and applying them to Mylar. She finds Mylar, including silver and copper, at an industrial plastics company. Among her favorites is a flannel-backed Mylar that is flexible and easily bent.

emulsion transfer

Polaroid emulsion transfer is a different process, which uses the fully developed <u>positive</u>. The layer of emulsion is soaked loose from the print in hot water, transferred to cloth, and brayered. It is less satisfactory for fabric because the emulsion tends to shrink as it dries. The transfers also tend to lift off the surface of the fabric with moisture. However, emulsion transfers work well on stable surfaces like heavy watercolor paper, wood, or Mylar.

Christine Mariotti
Polaroid transfer on silk
7¹/₂" x 6¹/₂"

After taking a color slide of a kimono, Christine placed the slide in the Vivitar for exposure onto Polaroid film. Once the print was transferred to silk, she worked on the surface of the print, adding lines with pens and markers, and then adding gold paint.

Christine Mariotti
Polaroid emulsion transfer on silk
7¹/₂" x 6¹/₂"

The emulsion transfer process, a variation of the Polaroid transfer, was used to print the photograph of a woman wearing a kimono. Folds in the emulsion create fine lines of pattern in the transfer. As the emulsion is lifted, it can be distorted to create the edge patterns.

additional help

Acetate: See Transparency.

Acetone: See Solvents and Propellants.

Acrylics: Acrylic paints are pigments in an acrylic polymer emulsion. They can be thinned with water or acrylic medium and can be cleaned up with water immediately, but cure or harden to water-fastness. Acrylics are more opaque than textile paints and cause some stiffening of the fabric. They require a transparent base to give them the consistency needed for screening. No heat setting is required. Acrylics are used for printing, stamping, painting, or stenciling.

Airbrush: A process which uses compressed air for spraying liquid paints. Textile airbrush inks can be used with any standard airbrush. A simple, convenient airbrush called the Air Marker utilizes the Letrajet™, a device which connects a Pantone® fine-tipped marker to canned propellant (Letraset's propellant or Badger's Propel). A fine spray is produced from a wide range of colors. As an alternative, Carnival produces a textile dye in spray cans called Dye*namite™. An atomizer or a small hand-held spray gun provides an inexpensive alternative to airbrush. The spray is not as consistent, but with practice you will get good results. Use airbrush ink or textile paint smoothed to a consistency which will move easily through the sprayer.

Airbrush Inks for Textiles: Special inks, made for airbrushing, are thinner than textile paint, but are as intense in color and can be used to paint or stamp color directly onto fabric.

Altered Images: Once you have copied a photograph you're ready for the fun of introducing changes. Transform you husband into Mr. America by pasting his head onto a muscleman's body. With a quick snip, remove a political incompetent from the scene. Insert a friend's image standing upright on a horse as it vaults over a water jump. Put yourself at the North Pole, sitting on the Eiffel Tower, or leaping over the Golden Gate Bridge. I placed Mozart under one of my quilts with this snipping process. Stacking transparencies allows further image play. Overlay your portrait with the things filling your head on any given day—dreams, birds, bats, feathers, or heavy thoughts.

Block-out: A block-out intercepts light to prevent exposure, or inhibits the transfer of paint, as with a resist. A paper star used in the direct-contact frame becomes a block-out. A star drawn on a transparency makes a linear block-out. Your hand, placed on any sensitized fabric during exposure, becomes the block-out. Block-out designs can be applied to a transparent material (glass, tracing paper, clear plastic bag) for use in making an exposure.

Blueprint: See Cyanotype.

Brayer: This simple tool consists of a free-turning hard rubber, plastic, or foam cylinder, 2" to 5" wide, with a handle. It is like a small paint roller and is used to exert even pressure over a flat area.

Brownprint: See Van Dyke

Burnish: To rub with pressure over a surface, usually with a hard wood or metal tool. Burnishing aids in transfer.

Centering (aligning) prints on fabric: See Registration.

Collograph: A print from a collograph plate (a linoleum block, for example, with textures adhered to the surface). The collage is sealed to make it resistant to the paint used.

Clear Wrap: Transparent plastic kitchen wrap (Handiwrap® or Saran Wrap™) is used in the studio to protect surfaces from wet inks or paints. It offers see-through protection from moisture, and retards drying time when used as a cover.

Contact Frame: See Direct-Contact Frame.

Contact Paper: Self-adhesive paper made for household use. Common brands are Con-Tact, Magic Paper, and Grid-Grip™. It consists of an adhesive plastic layer with a waxed-paper-like backing, and the sheets can be separated for silk-screen printing, stencils, etc. The translucent ones are preferred over the opaques for most craft uses.

Copy Transfer: The process of transferring either a color or a black and white copy from a sheet of paper to fabric by any of a variety of means (e.g., hot iron, solvent, transfer sheets, contact paper, etc.).

Crayons: See Transfer Crayons.

Cut-outs: Figures, letters, or images cut from paper (or anything similar) can be used as block-outs for screen printing, or as stencils with dye transfer or light-sensitive methods. See also Block-outs.

Cyanotype (Blueprint): A process in which cloth is saturated with iron-bearing compounds which make it sensitive to ultra-violet (UV) light. A block-out (photo-negative, leaves, cut-outs, etc.) is then used to protect parts of the cloth from exposure to light. Exposed areas develop the characteristic blue color, while unexposed areas wash out to the original fabric color.

Darkroom: Any room essentially free of outdoor light can be used for light-sensitive processes. Blueprinting and photo-screen printing require low lighting for preparation, and a darkroom only for drying. A closet (with a towel to block light from coming in under the door) will work. A cupboard or drawer is adequate to dry a screen. Closing doors and covering windows in black plastic can turn a shop, laundry room, or small work area into a darkroom. Use a bathroom, but only if you have another. It is best not to do this work in the living areas of your home. For a work light, use a photo-safe light, a 75-watt yellow bulb, or a 25-watt incandescent bulb. Keep your bulb, black plastic, clothesline, and masking tape together in a box or drawer so you can reconstruct your darkroom in minutes.

Direct-Contact Frame: A set-up to provide direct contact between sensitized material and a block-out design for exposure to light. You can make an inexpensive direct-contact frame consisting of a piece of wood (Masonite, plywood, or an abandoned breadboard), $1/2$" to 1"-thick flexible foam pad, black fabric, and a sheet of Plexiglas or glass. All layers should be a couple of inches larger than the largest negative or design you intend to use. The black fabric protects the sensitized fabric before exposure or covers the foam during exposure. The layers must fit tightly so that no light can filter through. For light-sensitive printing the black fabric and foam pad are not necessary.

Disperse Dyes: Disperse (sublimation) dyes bond permanently with synthetic fabrics at relatively low temperatures, making them convenient for home use. They change from a solid to a gaseous state with the application of heat and pressure. During heat setting fibers expand or open to capture the fumes given off as the dyes sublime. Available in liquid form (Deka Iron-On), or powder form (PRO Chemical or Aljo), they can be mixed and painted to make dye sheets. The colors are fast to light and water on the appropriate fabrics. Care must be taken to avoid any breathing of the disperse dye powders.

Disposal: Be environmentally responsible. Read all labels and dispose of materials only as directed. While information and directions are offered in this text, remember that regulations change from state to state, and even from county to county. For help, call your fire department, your local toxic waste disposal management, or the Department of Fish and Wildlife. Request Material Safety Data Sheets when you purchase anything potentially hazardous. Small amounts of the solutions used in this book can be disposed of by diluting ($1/2$ cup solution to a gallon of water) and flushing them down the drain with lots of water. I mix only the amount of chemicals or solutions needed to avoid disposal. The amounts used in single projects are regarded as minimal. For large amounts (production or classes) it will be important to check with your local agencies. See also Hazardous Materials. Never dispose of one chemical immediately after another down a drain (even diluted), since this can cause a reaction, particularly with an acid and a base. Never pour any chemicals into the ground. Always clearly label chemicals being stored.

Dye Sticks: Made by Pentel, these easy-to-use colors are for direct use on cloth. When heat set they are permanent on cottons.

Dye Transfer: The process of transferring disperse dyes to synthetic fabric using heat. Dye transfer is also what happens in the laundry when your white blouse gets washed with something green. See also Disperse Dyes.

Dye Transfer Papers (or Dye Transfer Sheets): Sheets of paper painted with liquid disperse dyes and used for transfer. See also Disperse Dyes.

Extender: A translucent medium with a paint-like consistency without pigment or dye. Also called transparent base. In silk-screening it is used to dilute a color's intensity without making it more liquid or runny.

Fabric Crayons: See Transfer Crayons.

Fabric Finishes: Treatments are often applied to fabrics to make them wrinkle-free, crease-resistant, water-resistant, glazed, or polished, any of which may interfere with dye absorption. See also PFP Fabrics.

Foamboard: A rigid white foam core panel, available in various thickness, coated on both sides with white or colored paper. It is easily cut and lightweight. For most craft uses, the $3/16$" or $1/4$" thickness is adequate.

Foamcore: See Foamboard.

Freezer Paper: A plastic surfaced paper, made originally to wrap meat for freezing. It can be used as a stabilizer for running fabric through a printer or copier, or as a stencil for quick-screening, painting, or spraying. The papers are made by Reynolds®, Magic Wrap, and Grid-Grip, and are available by the roll in some grocery or hardware stores. For stencils, the plasticized side of the paper is ironed onto fabric with a medium hot iron.

Generation Copies: A first photocopy of any material is referred to as the first-generation copy. A copy made from the copy is a second-generation copy. As copying proceeds through generations, clarity and detail are lost. Therefore, first-generation copies are always best for use in transfers.

Glass: A picture-framing shop or glass company will cut glass to size, and many carry pre-cut glass in standard sizes. Cut edges should be ground smooth, or covered with tape. Store glass on edge. Non-glare glass is not essential, but is easier to work with in bright sunshine. Plexiglas also works, is non-breakable, and its edges pose no hazard.

Halftone Negative: See Negative

Hand Painting: All heat-set water-based textile paints or textile airbrush inks can be used for hand painting, either thinned or thickened. Use a palette (a disposable plastic tray or plate), adding small dabs of color. A flat-tipped, oil-painting brush with some stiffness works well, and pointed brushes will be needed for tiny details.

Thinned Color: Thin paint with water and apply like watercolor. Place fabric print over absorbent paper, brush color onto a small area, and constantly blot to prevent bleeding. Paint one area, then heat set. If the color is too pale, paint it again.

Thickened color: Mix textile color with extender and paint an even layer onto the fabric. It will not be necessary to blot, as colors will not spread or run. However, this thicker paint is more difficult to manipulate and slower to dry.

Hazardous Materials: The Federal Hazardous Substances Act requires labeling of all consumer art and craft materials which are potentially hazardous. Always request a Material Safety Data Sheet from the manufacturer. The designations DANGER, WARNING, or CAUTION must be used, and the label must list what the hazardous ingredients are, what precautions to take, and the recommended first-aid treatment. NO processes in this book use materials labeled DANGER, the most extreme of the three. Always read the label and WARNING or CAUTION information before use.

Good references for fiber artists are the books (listed in the Bibliography) by Michael McCann and by Shaw and Rossol. It is important to know and understand the materials you work with so that you can handle them intelligently and safely. A few good general rules for everyone are:

1. Never use hazardous substances in your kitchen.
2. Reserve measuring or mixing utensils for craft use only, and never mix them with kitchen ware.
3. Work with adequate ventilation, outdoors when recommended.
4. Allow no food, drink, children, or open flames near any potentially hazardous material.
5. Use masks, gloves, and safe-box when recommended.
6. Wash your hands and work surfaces thoroughly when you have finished, then change clothes. See also Disposal.

Heat Setting: A process used to set paints and to make transfers. To add permanence to water-based textile paints, dry the print, then heat set by ironing for 20 to 30 seconds (or follow manufacturers directions). If you iron on the reverse side, or use a press cloth, double the time. If patience isn't one of your virtues, you are familiar with the sizzling of a hot iron on wet dye. Keep an iron for heat setting only. Dyes burned onto the plate of an iron always let go at inappropriate moments (usually on new white shirts, and never on old ones you don't give two hoots about). Use as hot an iron as the fabric will allow. Fabrics which cannot tolerate 250° F should not be used if you want permanence. Drying or curing prints in sunlight before heat setting increases permanence. Allow several days before washing. Heat setting is also used in various transfers, either by heat press or by a hot iron combined with pressure.

Inkodye: A light-sensitive permanent vat dye in a leuco-base, which means the color is not evident until it is developed or exposed to sunlight or ironing (sunlight produces brighter colors). It is used for printing, stamping, dyeing, and screen printing on cotton, linen, and viscose rayon. Shelf life, if stored in subdued light, is six months to a year. Some vat dyes now have enough pigment added so that colors can be visually identified. Fabrics coated with light-sensitive Inkodye can be used in direct contact prints, in a process similar to blueprinting (called Inko printing). Inkodyes must be handled carefully and used outdoors (where you would do photograms or Inko prints anyway), as good ventilation is a must. Purchase liquid dyes to avoid handling and measuring powders. If you do use powders, a North respirator is recommended.

Iron and Board: Reserve an iron especially for heat setting paints and dyes. Use a non-steam iron with a flat sole-plate; steam vents leave dots of undeveloped color during heat setting. A thrift shop or garage sale is a good source. A few craft suppliers sell new ones as "specialty" items. An old breadboard covered with padding and fabric can be kept just for heat setting dyes. Add a new fabric layer as needed.

Kwik-Print: A printing method in which fabric is painted with a light-sensitive color, covered with a block-out, and exposed to sunlight. Color develops in the exposed areas, and washes out in the protected areas. It is available in a variety of colors.

Kodalith: A film positive in which all grays are turned into either black or white (a halftone is a positive in which grays are turned into patterns of dots). Also called a line film positive, a Kodalith can be printed on transparent acetate. Contact prints made from high-contrast Kodaliths are sharp and clear. If your photo image is clear, it can be copied onto a transparency and used in a contact print. If the image is unclear or lacks strong dark/light contrast, have a photo lab make a Kodalith or high-contrast positive from your image.

Laminated Fabric: A fabric which has been bonded to a paper backing such as iron-on freezer paper. The rigidity added by laminating makes the paper easier to handle on copiers, some printers, and for painting.

Lettering: With words and letters fabric creations are converted into documents, announcements, and personal commentary. Any process in this book can be used with lettering as the image. A permanent marker, used directly on fabric, is the most obvious means of lettering. Markers on acetate sheets can be used for exposure for cyanotype and photo silk-screen. Rubber stamps allow for lines which meander, turn corners, or move in irregular lines. For exact spacing and text, use the computer. Remember that a one-step transfer creates a mirror image (or reversal).

Mineral Spirits: See Solvents and Propellants

Mirror Image: See Reversal

Natural Forms: Anything from nature. Natural objects (such as leaves, branches, pebbles, or sticks) which are opaque can be used as block-outs for light-sensitive processes. In dye transfer or stamping they can be used as the printing plates. Found objects, non-natural, or man-made forms (coins, raw spaghetti, string, tools, screen) are utilized in the same way.

Negative: A transparent image in which the photographic lights and darks are opposite those in nature. Negatives are used in light-sensitive processes in which the dark areas inhibit the passage of sunlight and do not develop. They therefore wash out after exposure, making a positive print. If a print from your negative is not distinct or clear, a halftone negative can be made at a photo lab. In a halftone, gray areas are translated to patterns of dots, which will produce a clearer image. A negative print refers to a background or reverse print. A blue sky, printed so that a white unprinted area is left in the shape of the bird, creates the bird as a negative shape. If the bird itself was printed, it would be a positive print. In a Polaroid transfer, when the film is separated, there is a positive (the half which is normally printed and viewed) and the negative (the half with the chemicals on it). See Halftone Negative.

Newsprint: Unprinted newspaper

Opaquer: Opaque liquids block out or conceal unwanted marks on a background. For copiers, opaquers are referred to as white-out or correction fluid. For screen printing or stenciling, they can be mixed with colors to make them more opaque and less transparent. Some make paint dry faster (in the screen). See Printing on Dark Fabric.

Original: In the context of this book, an original is the image which is going to be printed or transferred. Thus, the original may actually be a copy or a composite paste-up design from which a transfer is to be made. It is the starting point of the printing process.

Paints: See Textile Paints.

Permanent Markers: Felt-tipped marking pens (identified as permanent) contain ink which will not wash out of fabric. Available in a wide range of colors with wide, pointed, or brush tips, my favorites include Marvy Fabric Markers, Fabricmate, and Pigma Micron. For permanent black markers, try Sanford's Sharpie, Pilot's SC-UF, or the Finepoint System markers which come in various point sizes. Fabricmates (heat setting recommended) come in brights and pastels, and the Pigma Microns make very fine lines. Marks-a-Lot® are very permanent wide-point markers. Marvys give brilliant color without streaks. While markers are easy to use, it is difficult to blend colors or avoid stroke lines. Always test markers, as even "permanent" ones may bleed on treated or synthetic fibers. I heat set all work with markers.

PFP Fabrics: PFP fabrics are those which have been Prepared For Printing. Since finishes can interfere with the penetration or absorption of dyes, the best results are achieved on scoured or degummed and/or bleached fabrics. Invisible lubricants, oil, dust, and impurities all may interfere with dye absorbency. Starch, glaze, or sizing left in fabric will absorb dye or paint. When laundered, these fillers wash out, and dye goes with them. Special untreated fabrics, made for dyers and printers, are available from Testfabrics, Inc. Treatments for wrinkle-resistance, water-repellence, permanent press, drip-dry, glazing, and soil resistance will not wash out easily, and some treatments won't budge. Because cottons wrinkle, they are subjected to the most surface treatments. To prepare fabric wash it with the following solution, using no additives such as water softeners, which may deposit a residue that interferes with dye absorption.

Recommended washing:

1/4 cup of Synthrapol
Washer load of water

One dye artist recommends boiling fabric for 2 to 4 hours in the following solution:
1 gallon of water per ounce of fabric
1 teaspoon of detergent
2 teaspoons of washing soda

Another formula calls for the following for each washing machine load:

$\frac{1}{4}$ cup of Synthrapol

$\frac{1}{4}$ cup of detergent

$\frac{1}{4}$ to $\frac{1}{2}$ cup of soda ash (similar to washing soda but without additives, available from pool suppliers or dye companies).

Photograms: Produced with light-sensitive processes, photograms are images exposed from objects rather than photographic transparencies.

Photo Transfer: Any method by which a photographic image is transferred to cloth (solvent transfer, thermal transfer sheets, dye transfer, Polaroid transfer, and others).

Positive: A film positive is a photographic image in which the lights and darks correspond to the original. The reverse of a negative, it consists of dark areas applied to a transparent sheet of acetate. A photographic film positive can be made by copying any photograph to a transparent sheet. A positive photocopy (on paper, not film) can be solvent-transferred to fabric, producing a mirror image. A positive photocopy on a transparency can be used for exposure with a photo silk-screen or thermo imager. In a positive print the original appears as the printed image. The image itself, not the background, is printed or developed. In Polaroid transfer, the positive is the half of the film sandwich that is normally viewed. See Kodalith.

Printing on Dark Fabric: Water-based textile paints work best when a dark or bright color is printed onto a light background. Printing light on dark is more difficult (it is like trying to dye a blue fabric yellow). Deka's opaque white (or covering white) can be mixed with colors to make them less transparent. PROfab makes an opaque white #101 to which color concentrates can be added for opaque color. Acrylic or opaque textile paints tend to dry on the surface rather than to soak into the fibers. Opaquers tend to be quick-drying. See also Opaquers.

Propellant: See Solvents and Propellants.

Registration: Any method used to align parts or colors of a print, or to produce an identical series. Aligning or registering is important for repeat units or when a print must parallel the grain of the fabric. Fabric is more difficult to register than paper, as it shrinks or warps slightly from the textile paint. Registration of a series requires both screen and fabric to be in the same exact place for each print. Registration for centering is accomplished by several methods: folding, marking, and with hinges or clamps.

Folding: For single prints, or for T-shirts and sweatshirts, crease the cloth both horizontally and vertically and press the folds lightly. Mark the center top and side of the designand carry those lines out to the screen print frame. Then align folds in fabric with marks on the frame. When these indicators line up, the print will be centered. For a freezer-paper stencil, fold both the fabric and paper at center then align the folds.

Marking: Place a smooth, clean cardboard on the printing area. Lay the prepared frame on top and, with a marking pen, draw a line around the edge of the frame on the cardboard. Make a print on the cardboard and lift the screen. Pat the print dry with paper towels. Place a pre-cut piece of thin muslin or light-colored cloth on the printed cardboard. You'll be able to see the image right through it. Center the cloth over the design, then mark a line to indicate the edges or corners of the cloth. Cut all the fabric on which you intend to print the same size as your muslin sample. Place the fabric in the marked area and place the frame back down in its marked position; the next image will duplicate the placement of the first. This is a very basic registration and it is all you'll need for single-color prints (or even a two- or three-color print) in a small series.

Hinges or Clamps: Some screen-printing frames come hinged to a wood panel. Use it for identical multiples. Hinges can be removed for free-hand printing. To add your own, use pin hinges—one set on your screen and a second aligned on a wood panel. To remove the screen for cleaning, withdraw the pins. Special clamps can be attached to a plywood panel and the frame can be slipped into the clamps and tightened into place. Two clamps go at one end of a frame and form a hinge. Also available is a metal arm for use with a hinged frame. It holds the screen up off the fabric between prints. A simple and inexpensive arm can be made from 5" to 6" of your wooden yardstick. Drill the stick and screw it to the side of the frame to serve as a crutch.

For random or all-over patterns, first print several of your images on paper, cut them out, and arrange them on your fabric. Then place the screen over a paper print, holding it just off the surface to visually align the screen with the paper print. Tilt the screen, keeping one edge on the fabric, and slip the paper out before printing. If the next print is close and the frame will touch wet paint, cover the paint with scrap paper to protect both print and frame.

Reversal: A reversal can be either of two changes that occur in printmaking. One reversal is the mirror image of an original; the other is between light and dark, or positive and negative. Mirror-image reversals occur in one-step transfer methods. For example, solvent transfer of black and white copies and thermal transfer of color are both reversal methods. In each case, lettering will transfer backwards, images reverse, and your hair will appear to be parted on the other side. In resist methods, we get another kind of reversal. In cyanotype a negative is needed to produce a positive image in the blue print. A photogram, which uses a positive, produces a negative image.

Safety: See Hazardous Materials.

Sensitizers: Chemicals used in photo emulsion for screen printing, and in light-sensitive liquids for cyanotype, Van Dyke, Kwik-Print, or Inko prints. They make the fabric receptive to light, which develops the sensitized cloth. All sensitizers must be used with caution. Read all warnings and follow all directions carefully.

Second Transfers: Once an image has been transferred, a second transfer can sometimes be made, although it is never as brilliant as the first. Crayon transfer, computer heat-transfer ribbon, and dye papers can all be used to make multiple prints of diminishing intensity.

Solvents and Propellants: Solvents are used to dissolve and transport ink or toner in copy transfer. All solvents pose some health or safety hazard. Use outdoors or with a hooded vent, and away from open flames. Mineral spirits is combustible, turpentine is flammable, and acetone is highly flammable. Turpentine, a common workshop solvent, is hazardous through skin contact, inhalation, and ingestion. If you have small children in your house, don't have turpentine. Mineral spirits and acetone are both slightly toxic. The specific uses of each are covered in Solvent Transfer on pages 17-18. The solvents present in some permanent marking pens must be used with adequate ventilation. Look for non-toxic inks, read the labels on markers, and know what you are using. Sprays often contain propellants which serve to evenly distribute solvents or paint from a spray can. Particles can remain in the air for hours after spraying. Use them only outdoors or with adequate venting. When another product will work, avoid aerosol sprays.

Spray Adhesive: An aerosol adhesive used to mount photographs or artwork, usually sprayed to each of two surfaces before joining. It makes a smooth bond, but must be used outdoors. Read labels carefully and avoid breathing the mist. Wear a mask.

Stabilized Fabric: Any fabric attached to a backing, such as freezer paper, for use in a copier or printer, or fabric which has been stiffened or reinforced with alginate, spray starch, etc. See pages 10-11 in Chapter 1 for a detailed discussion. See also Freezer Paper.

Stencil: A stencil is any thin, flat surface material used to prevent paint from spreading into a protected area. In quick-screen, freezer paper becomes the stencil. Contact paper, photo emulsion, newsprint, acetate, stickers, or tape are all used as stencils. See also Block-outs.

Sublimation Dyes: See Disperse Dyes.

Textile Paints: Any paint identified as a water-based textile paint will work for most processes in this book. A few of the commonly used brands include Versatex, PROfab, Lumière, Deka, Neopaque, Speedball, and Createx. Colors can be mixed to produce tints, shades, and combinations. Deka makes a metallic paint that is good for painting or stenciling, but the particles will not go through a 14xx silk screen mesh. Lumière Fabric Paints are available as opalescents or metallics and are opaque on dark fabrics. Water-based fabric paints need heat setting, though some will cure with air drying. Drying in direct sunlight before heat setting increases permanence. Allow several days of curing before washing. If dyes are used, such as Procion or Inko, a thickener will be needed to achieve the right consistency for screening. Dyes are sometimes preferred by designers because they do not alter the feel (or hand) of the fabric. Dye is absorbed by the fibers and does not sit on the surface. Acrylic paints (which are very opaque) have some desirable visual qualities, but they are difficult to sew through and leave needle holes. Airbrush inks for textiles are intense in color, but thinner, and work well for direct painting or stamping.

Thermal Imager: Either of two machines (thermal imager or Print Gocco) in which light or heat reacts with carbon to etch an image onto a special mesh or screen. Any image run through a copier has adequate carbon to be used. In the thermal imager, a quartz light is used—in Print Gocco, a flashbulb.

Thermal Screen: A finely woven synthetic mesh coated with a thin plastic surface. It is etched in a thermal imager.

Transfer Crayons: Heat transfer crayons are made for use on paper to be transferred by heat setting to fabric. They contain disperse dyes and work best on synthetic fabrics.

Transparency: A clear plastic sheet onto which an image can be transferred (in a copier or printer), or to which opaque papers or inks can be applied. In a copy shop ask for an acetate or transparency for the overhead projector. They are sold as single sheets or by the box. For the photocopier, it is essential to find a compatible transparency. Transparency boxes list the specific machines in which they can be used. The heat generated by machines varies, as do the levels of heat tolerance of the transparencies. Using the incorrect transparency may cause it to overheat and warp, distorting the image. Or, even worse, it may melt in the machine. Think of your machine as a picky eater. Feed the machine the right papers, and all runs smoothly. Feed it something disagreeable, and there will be interior rumblings. Designs on transparencies must be opaque to produce clear prints. Two stacked transparencies will be more opaque than one. Tape perfectly aligned edges with clear tape and use this double layer for photo-emulsion exposure. There are transparency sheets for both laser and inkjet printers as well as copiers. Make all corrections or alterations on your copies (a ladybug can be enlarged to grade B movie proportions). Make only the final copy on a transparency for a contact print.

Transparent Base: See Extender.

Untreated Cloth: See PFP Fabrics.

Van Dyke Print: A light-sensitive print which is brown in color; also, a variation of cyanotype in which the blue print is subjected to a tannic acid solution, which produces the brown tones.

Well: A space on a screen printing frame reserved to hold paint during printing. A stencil which covers the entire screen forms its own well. On other screens, masking tape or contact paper is applied to the edges to reserve the space.

resource guide

1. Art supply store
2. Copy shop
3. Craft and hobby store
4. Fabric or quilt shop
5. Hardware store
6. Office supply store
7. School supply store
8. Rubber stamp shop
9. Health food store

10. Aljo Manufacturing Company
    81-83 Franklin Street
    NY, NY 10013
    212 226-2878

11. Air Waves
    7787 Graphics Way
    Lewis Center, Ohio 43035
    800 818-2366

12. BlackLightning, Inc.
    Riddlepond Road
    West Topsham, VT 05086
    800 252-2599
    802 439-6463 fax
    e-mail: sales@flashmag.com

13. Bryant Laboratory, Inc.
    1101 Fifth Street
    Berkeley, CA 94710
    510 526-3141

14. Blueprints - Printables
    1400 "A" Marsten Road
    Burlingame, CA 94010
    415 348-2600
    415 348-2888 fax

15. Calcom
    2836 10th Street
    Berkeley, CA 94710
    510 841-7477

16. Clotilde Inc.
    B-3000
    Louisiana, MO 63353-3000
    800 772-2891

17. Computer Friends, Inc.
    13865 N.W. Cornell
    Portland, OR 97229
    800 547-3303
    503 643-5379 fax
    e-mail: Cfriends@teleport.com

18. Connections Catalog
    3065 Research Drive
    Richmond, CA 94806
    800 643-0800
    510 223-6313

19. Daniel Smith
    P.O. Box 84268
    4130 First Avenue South
    Seattle, WA 98124-5568
    800 426-6740
    800 238-4065 fax

20. Data Image
    13175 Monterey Highway, Suite A
    San Martin, CA 95046
    408 686-9065
    408 686-9066 fax

21. Dharma Trading Co.
    P.O. Box 150916
    San Rafael, CA 94915
    800 542-5227

22. Dick Blick
    P.O. Box 1267
    Galesburg, IL 61402
    800 634-7001

23. Earth Guild
    33 Haywood Street
    Asheville, NC 28801
    800 327-8448
    704 255-8593 fax
    e-mail: catalog@earthguild.com
    www.earthguild.com

24. G & S Dye and Accessories Ltd.
    300 Steelcase Road W., #19
    Markham, ON L3R 2W2
    800 596-0550
    e-mail: gsdye/paro

25. Gramma's Graphics, Inc.
    20 Birling Gap, IOFA-P7
    Fairport, NY 14450
    716 223-4309
    716 223-4789 fax
    www.computer-connection.net/~dounelly

26. Hanes T-Shirt Maker
    6600 Silacci Way
    Gilroy, CA 95020
    888 828-4534
    www.hanes2u.com

27. Imagination Station
    7571 Crater Lake Highway, Suite #101
    White City, OR 97503
    541 826-7954
    800 338-3857

28. Jones Tones
    33865 United Avenue
    Pueblo, CO 81001
    800 397 9667
    719 948-3348 fax

29. Photographers' Formulary
    P.O. Box 950
    Condon, MT 59826
    800 922-5255
    406 754-2896 fax

30. Photo Textiles
    P.O. Box 3063
    Bloomington, IN 47402-3063
    800 388-3961

31. PRO Chemical & Dye, Inc.
    P.O. Box 14
    Somerset, MA 02726
    508 676-3838
    800 228-9393

32. Rockland Colloid Corp.
    P.O. Box 376
    Piermont, NY 10968
    914 359-5559
    914 365-6663 fax
    info@rockaloid.com

33. Rupert, Gibbon & Spider Inc.
    P.O. Box 425
    Healdsburg, CA 95448
    800 442-0455
    707 433-9577
    707 433-4906 fax
    jacquard@sonic.net

34. Sax Arts and Crafts
    P.O. Box 51710
    New Berlin, WI 53151
    800 558-6696

35. Screen Process Supplies Mfg. Co.
    530 Mac Donald Ave.
    Richmond, CA 94801
    510 235-8330

36. Siphon Art Products
    P.O. Box 150710
    San Rafael, CA 94915-0710
    510 236-0949

37. Stahls' Inc.
    20600 Stephens Street
    St. Claire Shores, MI 48080
    800 622-2264
    800 346-2216 fax

38. Testfabrics, Inc.
    P.O. Box 26
    West Pittston, PA 18643
    717 603-0432
    717 603-0433 fax

39. Thai Silks
    252 F State Street
    Los Altos, CA 94022
    800 221-SILK

40. Texicolor Corporation, Inc.
    444 Castro Street, Suite 425
    Mountain View, CA 94041-2053
    415 968-8183
    415 968-8184 fax

41. Welsh Products, Inc.
    P.O. Box 845
    Benicia, CA 94510
    800 745-3255
    707 745-3252
    707 745-0330 fax
    e-mail: welshpi@ix.netcom.com

index

bibliography

Books

Croner, Marjorie. *Fabric Photos*. Loveland, CO: Interweave Press, 1989.

Quilt National Exhibit Catalog. The Dairy Barn. Athens, OH.

Dunnewold, Jane. *Complex Cloth*. Bothell, WA: That Patchwork Place, Inc. 1996.

Hewitt, Barbara. *Blueprints on Fabric*. Loveland, CO: Interweave Press, Inc. 1995.

Howell-Koehler, Nancy. *Photo Art Processes*. Worcester, MA: Davis Publication, Inc., 1980.

Laury, Jean Ray. *Imagery on Fabric*. Lafayette, CA: C&T Publishing, 1993.

Laury, Jean Ray. *No Dragons on My Quilt*. Paducah, KY: American Quilter's Society, 1990.

McCann, Michael. *Artist Beware*. New York: Watson-Guptill, 1979.

McCann, Michael. *Health Hazards Manual for Artists*. New York; Nick Lyons Books,
   3rd edition, 1985.

Nature Printing Society. *The Art of Printing From Nature*: A Guide Book. Available from N.P.S. Editor,
   Sonja Larsen, 7675 Interlacken Road, Lark Shore, MN 56458

Nettles, Bea. *Breaking the Rules*: A Photo Media Cookbook. Urbana, IL: Inky Press Publication,
   2nd edition, 1987.

Polaroid Corporation. *Polaroid Guide to Instant Imaging*. Cambridge, MA. 800 225-1618

Shaw, Susan D. and Monona Rossal. *OvereXposure: Health Hazards in Photography*. New York, NY:
   Allworth Press, 2nd edition, 1991.

Simms, Ami. *Creating Scrapbook Quilts*. Flint, MI: Mallary Press, 1993.

Stocksdale, Joy. *Polychromatic Screen Printing*. City: Oregon Street Press, 1984.

Swedlund, Charles and Elizabeth. *Kwik Print*. Rochester, NY: Light Impressions Corp., 1989.

Quilt San Diego. *Visions: Quilt Art*. Lafayette, CA: C&T Publishing, 1996.

Westphal, Katherine. (introduction) *The Surface Designer's Handbook*, Asheville, NC:
   Lark Books, 1993.

Periodicals

Art/Quilt Magazine. Dept. S, P.O. Box 630927, Houston, TX 77263-0927 #713 975-6072 fax

Fiberarts. 50 College Street, Asherville, NC 28801, #704 253-0467

Rubberstampmadness. P.O. Box 610, Corvallis, OR 97339-0610 #541-752-0075

Surface Design Journal. P.O. Box 20799, Oakland, CA 94620 #510 841-2008

Threads Magazine. Taunton Press, Inc. 63 South Main Street, Newtown, CT 06470 #203 426-8171

Vamp Stamp News. P.O. Box 386, Hanover, MD 21076-0386 #410-760-3377

Jean Ray Laury is an internationally known quiltmaker and teacher, as well as the author of several books. Surface design has been a focus of Jean's work and teaching for many years. She is well-known for her originality, as well as for her ability to clarify and simplify every technique she teaches. Jean's clarity of presentation, enthusiasm for her processes, and humor make her classes favorites at seminars and conferences all over the country. Her quilts are non-conventional, very individual, and often humorous or political.

Jean received the 1997 Silver Star Award for lifetime achievement from Quilts Inc., and was honored at International Quilt Festival in Houston, Texas, in October 1997. She was named to the Quilters' Hall of Fame in 1982. She has received a California State Arts Commission grant, the Fresno Women Making History award, and an Outstanding Community Service award. She was honored by the San Francisco Women's Foundation for her contributions to the arts. Her work has been exhibited at the Museum of American Crafts in New York, the American Crayon Company, the DeYoung Museum (San Francisco), the Fresno Art Museum, California State University, and as part of many group shows. One of her quilts resides in the traveling Smithsonian exhibit, "Full Deck Art Quilts."

After completing a BA in Art and English at University of Northern Iowa, she taught art in junior high and high school, and at the university level. At graduate school at Stanford University, Jean discovered quilting and made her first quilt as part of a masters degree project. She then started teaching adult women in seminars and guilds (her favorite work).

Jean's books, articles, exhibitions, and lectures reflect her enjoyment of teaching, screen printing, and quiltmaking. Her workshops have taken her to many countries on five continents. She and Frank Laury live in the foothills of the California Sierras near Clovis and have two grown children. They are surrounded by woods, a creek, and an abundant array of birds and animals.

Other fine books by C&T Publishing

Anatomy of a Doll: The Fabric Sculptor's Handbook, Susanna Oroyan

Appliqué 12 Easy Ways! Elly Sienkiewicz

Art & Inspiration: Ruth B. McDowell, Ruth B. McDowell

The Art of Silk Ribbon Embroidery, Judith Baker Montano

The Artful Ribbon, Candace Kling

Baltimore Beauties and Beyond (Volume I), Elly Sienkiewicz

Basic Seminole Patchwork, Cheryl Greider Bradkin

Beyond the Horizon: Small Landscape Appliqué, Valerie Hearder

Crazy Quilt Handbook, Judith Montano

Crazy with Cotton, Diana Leone

88 Leaders in the Quilt World Today, Nihon Vogue Co., Ltd.

Elegant Stitches: An Illustrated Stitch Guide & Source Book of Inspiration, Judith Baker Montano

Enduring Grace: Quilts from the Shelburne Museum Collection, Celia Y. Oliver

The Fabric Makes the Quilt, Roberta Horton

Faces & Places: Images in Appliqué, Charlotte Warr Andersen

Fantastic Figures: Ideas & Techniques Using the New Clays, Susanna Oroyan

Fractured Landscape Quilts, Katie Pasquini Masopust

From Fiber to Fabric: The Essential Guide to Quiltmaking Textiles, Harriet Hargrave

Heirloom Machine Quilting, Third Edition, Harriet Hargrave

Impressionist Palette, Gai Perry

Judith Baker Montano: Art & Inspirations, Judith B. Montano

Kaleidoscopes & Quilts, Paula Nadelstern

The Magical Effects of Color, Joen Wolfrom

On the Surface: Thread Embellishment & Fabric Manipulation, Wendy Hill

Patchwork Persuasion: Fascinating Quilts from Traditional Designs, Joen Wolfrom

Quilts from the Civil War: Nine Projects, Historical Notes, Diary Entries, Barbara Brackman

Quilts, Quilts, and More Quilts! Diana McClun and Laura Nownes

Say It with Quilts, Diana McClun and Laura Nownes

Six Color World: Color, Cloth, Quilts & Wearables, Yvonne Porcella

Soft-Edge Piecing, Jinny Beyer

Start Quilting with Alex Anderson: Six Projects for First-Time Quilters, Alex Anderson

Tradition with a Twist: Variations on Your Favorite Quilts, Blanche Young and Dalene Young Stone

Trapunto by Machine, Hari Walner

The Visual Dance: Creating Spectacular Quilts, Joen Wolfrom

Willowood: Further Adventures in Buttonhole Stitch Appliqué, Jean Wells

For more information write for a free catalog from:
C&T Publishing, Inc.
P.O. Box 1456
Lafayette, CA 94549
(800) 284-1114
http://www.ctpub.com